Published by Collins
An imprint of HarperCollins Publishers
Westerhill Road
Bishopbriggs
Glasgow G64 2QT
www.harpercollins.co.uk

In association with National Geographic Partners, LLC

NATIONAL GEOGRAPHIC and the Yellow Border Design are trademarks of
the National Geographic Society and used under license.

National Geographic Kids Weird But True & Design are trademarks of
National Geographic Society and used under license.

First published 2020

ISBN 978-0-00-839580-3

10 9 8 7 6 5 4 3 2 1

A catalogue record for this book is available from the British Library

Printed and bound in China by RR Donnelley APS Co Ltd.

If you would like to comment on any aspect of this book, please contact
us at the above address or online.
natgeokidsbooks.co.uk
collins.reference@harpercollins.co.uk

Paper from responsible sources

NATIONAL
GEOGRAPHIC
KiDS

weird but true!

2021

wild & wacky
facts & photos!

# Contents

# Amazing
# EARTH

The **RESIN** from the **DRAGON'S BLOOD TREE** is used as a **COLOURING AGENT** and is also believed to have **MEDICINAL PROPERTIES.**

# CHAPTER 1

**Swing by page 10 for more terrific tree facts.**

# Beautiful but DEADLY

## NACREOUS CLOUDS

are **rare** and **mesmerising** cloud formations with a **DANGEROUS DARK SIDE.**

Known as **polar stratospheric clouds,** these fussy phenomena only show up in very **specific conditions,** at high altitudes in cold places like **Canada, Iceland, Scandinavia** and **The Antarctic.**

Because they **glow** with such **pearly,** iridescent colours, nacreous clouds get their name from the word '**nacre**', which means '**mother of pearl**'.

Though this stunning **rainbow display** may look **magical,** some types of nacreous clouds are **very dangerous** for the environment, because they speed up **chemical reactions** that can destroy the protective **ozone layer** that keeps us safe from the Sun's harmful rays.

Nacreous clouds in The Antarctic

# TOTALLY TREE-MENDOUS

Let's take a look at some of the world's most intriguing trees...

**BRISTLECONE PINES** are native to western USA and are amongst the hardiest of trees, being resistant to rot, insects and extreme weather. These characteristics have helped some bristlecone pines survive for around 5,000 years!

**RAINBOW EUCALYPTUS** trees shed their bark in strips, revealing their trunk beneath. Depending on how long the trunk is exposed to the sun the more it changes colour, creating a vivid pattern.

## DRAGON'S BLOOD TREES

get their name from the resin inside their bark that is a rich red colour. The locals of Socotra Island, Yemen, rely on the resin to cure wounds, ulcers and to lower fevers. Not to mention, it is used in voodoo, alchemy and witchcraft, due to the belief that the resin is real dragon's blood!

## GRANDIDIER'S BAOBABS

are found at the centre of many aspects of Madagascan culture. They are a great source of food with their seeds being eaten with rice and their fruits made into juice. Their bark can be dried out and used for roofing and rope.

**Ryan Hickman** has been operating a **recycling business** since he was just **three years old.** Within a few years, he had recycled over **800,000 bottles** and **cans!**

**Bins are banned** in one school in Australia! Students' only options are **recycling stations, compost bins** or **taking rubbish home** to recycle, making them think more carefully about what **packaging** they bring to school.

CLIMATE CHANGE CHAMPIONS

**Farmers** in **Australia** have been feeding **pink seaweed** to **cows** to reduce the amount of **methane gas** produced when they **burp** and **fart!** (Which **could** make a **positive impact** on **climate change!**).

**Students** can't **graduate** from schools in the **Philippines** until they **plant at least 10 trees.** This new law will help get over **175 million** trees planted each year, and an estimated **525 billion trees** planted in **one generation!**

One **environmental group** in **Denmark** offers tourists **free kayaking tours** in exchange for them using **litter-pickers** to **clear up rubbish** along the way!

# Life AT THE NORTH POLE

**North Pole** is a town in **Alaska, USA,** with a population of just over **2,000 people.** Despite its name, the town is **1,700 miles** from Earth's geographic North Pole!

During **winter,** the sun rises at around 11 am and sets at 3 pm, so the North Pole residents only get around *four hours of daylight!*

It's always **Christmas** in North Pole! **All year round**, the town is covered in **Christmas decorations**, **candy canes** and **lights**.

The **largest fibreglass statue** of **Father Christmas** in the world can be found in North Pole, standing at just over **12 metres (40 feet) tall!**

Each year, hundreds of thousands of letters addressed to Santa Claus end up in North Pole, where 'Santa's helpers' reply to as many children as possible.

## Christmas-themed street names

are very common in North Pole. Names include **Kris Kringle Drive**, **Snowman Lane**, **St Nicholas Drive**, and **Santa Claus Lane!**

# STOP! stacking stones

Stone-stacking in Tenerife, Spain

'Stone-stacking' towers on beaches and in National Parks are popular with tourists, but they may soon be a thing of the past!

In places all around the world, including Australia, Iceland and Spain, visitors love to come and take photos with the curious stone towers, as well as building their own. 'What's wrong with that?' you might ask...

Well, conservationists have explained that towers like these can cause damage to the local environment because so many creatures use these stones as their homes. When tourists pile the rocks up, they don't just take away insects' houses or disturb bird's nesting sites, they scare away food sources (some animals love to eat bugs!) and can even change the health of the plant organisms that grow in the area.

So, have a good look while you can, because these stacked stone towers may very soon be illegal!

# MAGICAL minerals

These places may look **OUT OF THIS WORLD,** but they're all located here on Earth and all owe their rare features to humble minerals like salt.

**Lake Hillier** is a saline lake in Australia known for it's unusual (but beautiful) **pink water!** Some scientists think the coloration may be caused by **micro-algae!**

**Pamukkale** is a natural site in Turkey where hot water from natural springs cascades down white terraces formed by layers of a sedimentary mineral called travertine. The name 'pamukkale' means 'cotton palace' in Turkish!

**Salar de Uyuni,** Bolivia, is the world's largest salt flat. During the rainy season, it turns into 'the world's largest mirror', as the wet salt below reflects the sky above!

**Cave of the Crystals,** a cave in Chihuahua, Mexico, is home to some of the largest natural selenite crystals ever found! At a depth of 300 metres (984 feet), the temperatures in this deadly cave can reach up to 57°C (135°F)!

# PECULIAR
## place names

**KENTUCKY (USA)**
is home to many funny place names, including **Blandville, Monkey's Eyebrow, Oddville, Pig,** and **Possum Trot!**

## Taumatawhakatangihangakoauauotamateaturipu-kakapikimaungahoronukupokaiwhenuakitanatahu

is the name of a hill in New Zealand –
it's the **longest place name in the world!**

Taumatawhakatangihangakoauauotamateaturipukakapikimaungahoronukupokaiwhenuakitanatahu

**Popcorn** (USA), **Scone** (Australia), (United Kingdom) and **Double Head Cabbage** (Belize) are all **real place names!**

**Westward Ho!** (England), **Hamilton!** (USA) and **Saint-Louis-du-Ha! Ha!** (Quebec) and are some of the only **place names** to include **exclamation marks!**

WELCOME TO

**WESTWARD HO!**

PLEASE DRIVE CAREFULLY

**ORANGE** is a city located in **Orange County,** California, USA. It has **five sister cities** including **Orange, Australia** and **Orange, France!**

**FROME** (pronounced '*froom*') is one of the most mispronounced place names ever, according to **linguists!**

# Step back in
## TIME

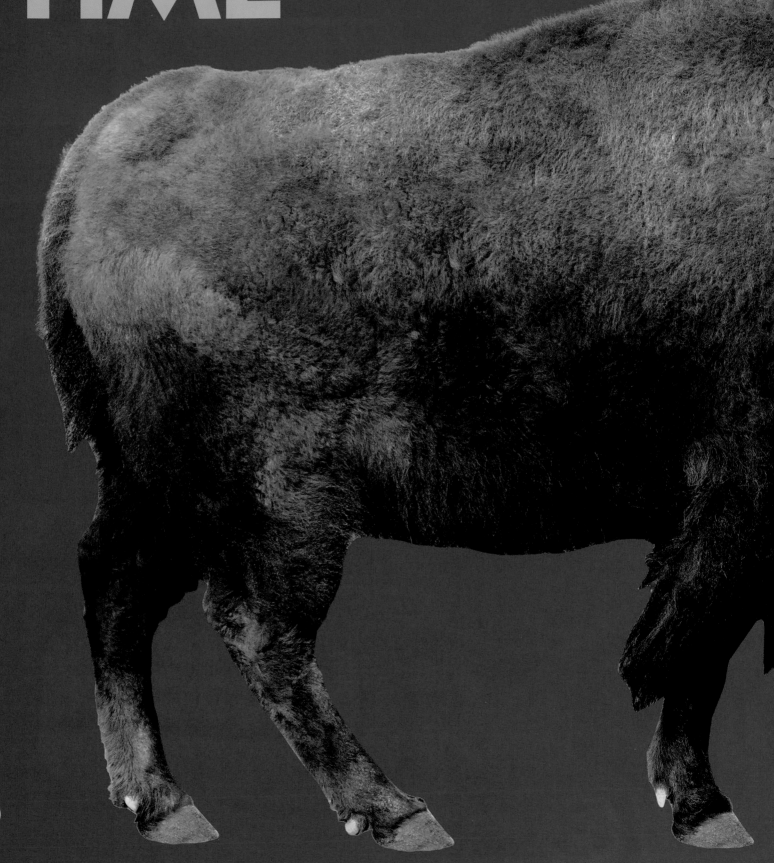

# CHAPTER 2

It is thought that **YELLOWSTONE NATIONAL PARK** is the only place in the **USA** where **BISON** have lived **CONTINUOUSLY** in the **WILD.**

Charge to page 24 for more about the bison's history.

# BISON Mania

**Bison** once covered the **Great Plains of America.** Back in the 18th century, there were over **60 million** of them!

Just **100 years later** though, less than **1,000 wild bison** were left – the entire species nearly became **extinct!** During the 19th century, bison **hunting** became a **craze** that grew to manic proportions. Over **50 million bison** were **hunted** for **food, hides** and for **sport.**

People used to **collect** bison **bones** left by hunters and **sell them.** Over one **13-year period,** an estimated **£1.9 million** worth of bison bones were bought in Kansas alone (that's around **31 million bison skeletons!**).

**Thankfully** for the bison, once the **trend** for hunting them started to **fade out,** some people set up **sanctuaries to protect** and **restore** the population. There are now approximately **18,000 bison** in the wild today, and while that's nowhere near the large quantities there used to be, they are **no longer an endangered species.**

## Totally **WEIRD!**

**Bison skulls** were used for all kinds of things, like refining **sugar,** creating **fine bone china,** and making **ink, glue,** or **plant fertiliser...**

# MAD medicines and CRAZY cures

Going to the **doctors** and going for a **haircut** may have taken you to the **same person** in the **1500s**. As many barbers had access to **straight razors**, they also trained to **perform** some minor **surgeries**.

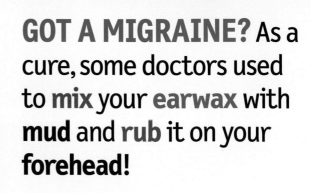

**GOT A MIGRAINE?** As a cure, some doctors used to **mix** your **earwax** with **mud** and **rub** it on your **forehead!**

**SNAILS** were used to treat **burns** in **medieval times!** People would **rub the snail** onto a burn to **heal it.** It may seem strange, but it has since been proven that **snail slime** really does have **healing properties!**

**POWDERED MUMMY** from **Egypt** was once popularly **prescribed** for **asthma** and **bruising**. And to **prevent puking**, you could expect to receive **second-hand nail clippings!**

**MEDICAL TREATMENTS** in the **1600s** often contained naturally occurring **poisons, fat, urine,** and **animal poo.**

# Voracious VICTORIANS

**QUEEN VICTORIA** could eat a seven course meal in just 30 minutes. Because her banquet guests were served after her and all plates were cleared as soon as she finished, some people never got to eat anything at all!

**MINCE PIES** were originally made with real meat in early Victorian recipes. They also used to be called 'mutton pies' or 'shrid pies.'

**JELLIED EELS** were a popular snack for the working-class in Victorian London. Eels from the River Thames contained natural gelatin, so they jellified when cooked.

**PINEAPPLES** were so rare in Victorian times that only extremely rich families could afford to grow them.

**POOR VICTORIANS** were so desperate for food that they would eat **broxy** – any meat that had come from a **diseased animal.**

**QUEEN VICTORIA** and **PRINCE ALBERT'S** giant royal wedding cake weighed over 130 kilograms – that's heavier than a panda! A preserved piece of the cake once sold at auction for £1,500!

# The History of holidays

## ROAM-ANS

Romans were the first civilisation to take holidays. Instead of going away for a week or two, Romans would 'roam' around for many years!

## GROUP TRAVEL

Henry VIII once took more than 3,000 people on holiday with him, including soldiers, his own cook and people to carry his 'luggage' of dishes, tapestries and beds!

## GOING UNDER

The Electric Seashore Tramroad (or 'Daddy Long Legs') was a railway carriage on 7-metre (23-feet) stilts that carried tourists along the shallow waters of Brighton beach!

## GOING UP

If you were wealthy enough and had a head for heights, then a trip to Egypt would have been perfect in years gone by (this photo was taken in 1893). Climbing the Pyramids of Giza is illegal nowadays, but it used to be a popular activity.

## PACKING LIGHT?

*Hints to Lady Travellers*, a book for female holiday-goers from 1889, suggested taking your own bath tub on holiday – and using it as a suitcase!

## GOING DOWN

The Sunken City of Baia used to be a luxurious holiday resort where rich Romans partied and relaxed in spas. Now underwater, tourists can snorkel among the ruins!

# PICCADILLY'S
## neverending NICKNAME

**PICCADILLY CIRCUS**
is an iconic area of London, most famously known for its ornate fountain and busy display of bright, neon signs.

'Piccadilly' sure is a funny name and there are many theories as to how it came about. The most widely known backstory is that a man named Robert Baker bought a small plot of land there back in 1612. Shortly after this, he became very successful in his business of making and selling 'piccadills' – huge, stiff lace collars that became very fashionable during the early 17th century!

**PICCADILLS** were super **fashionable**

After getting rich making his piccadill fortune, Robert Baker bought more land and constructed many buildings, including a mansion that the locals nicknamed 'Pickadilly Hall' behind his back. As we now know, the nickname well and truly stuck, as the area is still called Piccadilly today, over 400 years later!

# A PICTURE tells a THOUSAND WORDS

**CUNEIFORM** was one of the **earliest writing** systems ever used. Developed by Sumerians in ancient Mesopotamia (a historical region of western Asia) over 5,000 years ago, it probably first started out as **small pictures** that got simplified into symbols over time.

**HIEROGLYPHICS** were used for writing in Ancient Egypt for over 3,000 years. These pictorial symbols could be written **left to right, right to left,** or top to bottom!

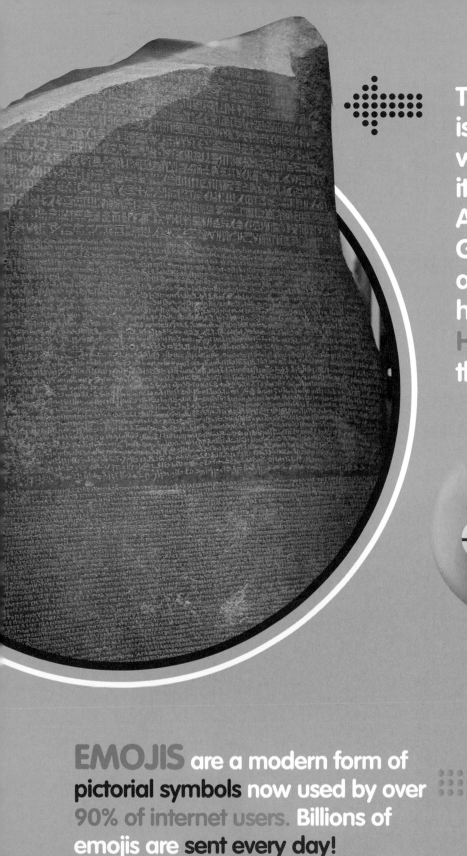

The **ROSETTA STONE** is a huge rock tablet inscribed with writing in 196 BC. Because it displayed the same text in Ancient Egyptian and Ancient Greek languages, it was an incredible discovery that helped historians to decipher Hieroglyphics. (After it took them 20 years to decode it!)

**EMOJIS** are a modern form of pictorial symbols now used by over 90% of internet users. Billions of emojis are sent every day!

## Totally **WEIRD!**

*MOBY DICK* was the **first book** to be **translated** into **emojis**. How do you think **historians of the future** will react to **discovering** and **decoding** that!?

# Carboniferous CURIOSITIES

The **CARBONIFEROUS PERIOD** (around **300 million years ago**) was named after the huge, carbon-rich swamp forests that eventually transformed into the **coal** we use today.

The **growth of so many trees** meant oxygen levels were nearly **50% higher** than they are now! This extra oxygen may have been the reason why so many creatures grew **EXTRA LARGE...**

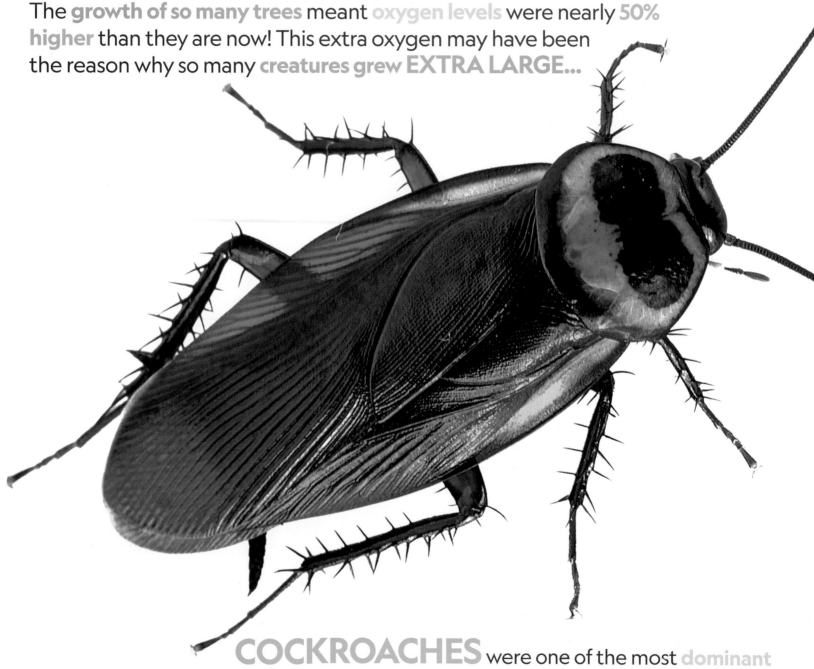

**COCKROACHES** were one of the most dominant insects back then. They grew up to **9 centimetres** (3.5 inches) long – **TWICE THE SIZE THEY ARE NOW!**

**MEGANEURA** were **giant, predatory, dragonfly-like creatures** thought to be the **largest-known flying insect species!** With wingspans of up to **70 centimetres** (28 inches), these 'dragonflies' were the size of some **hawks!**

**STETHACANTHUS** was a 'shark' with a very **peculiarly-shaped dorsal fin.** Just one example of why the Carboniferous Period was also known as the **'GOLDEN AGE OF SHARKS'!**

## Totally **WEIRD!**

**MEGARACHNE** were **giant sea scorpions** that grew to around the **size of dogs!** Their name means **'great spider'** because fossilised Megarachne were originally **misidentified** as giant spiders!

## ARTHROPLEURA

were **giant invertebrates** that looked like just **millipedes...** except they grew to the **size of cars!** They may have been the **LARGEST ARTHROPODS OF ALL TIME!**

**Amelia Earhart** was the **first solo female pilot** to complete a transatlantic flight. However, when she attempted to fly around the world in **1937** she disappeared and was **never found!**

# Mysterious

**Lucy Ann Johnson** was **found alive 52 years after** she first went **missing,** making hers one of the **longest disappearances ever!**

*The Mary Celeste* was an **abandoned ship** whose crew **completely disappeared in 1872.** No one knows what happened, but there were many **rumours** about **ghosts** and giant **squids!**

The '**Lost Colony**' was a group of **120 settlers** who mysteriously **vanished** from **Roanoke Island, USA,** in the **16th-century** without a **trace!**

**GEORGE WASHINGTON'S** false teeth went missing from the **National Museum of American History** in **1981.** Some teeth showed up a year later but others are **still missing!**

MRS. CHRISTIE FOUND
AT HARROGATE

Dramatic Re-union With Husband
in Famous Hydro.

"HER MEMORY GONE"

How Missing Novelist Spent Time While
Police and Public Looked for Her

Mrs. Christie, the missing inventor of detective stories, was traced last night to the Hydro, Harrogate, by her husband, Colonel Christie.

In an interview after a dramatic meeting between the pair, Colonel Christie told the DAILY HERALD that his wife had suffered from the " most complete loss of memory." She did not even recognise him, he added.

"She does not know why she is here."
—Col. Christie

Mrs. Christie          Col. Christie

**Slippery the Sea Lion** disappeared from a **sea park** in **Ontario, Canada** and was later found in **Ohio, USA.**

**Agatha Christie** was famous for **writing mystery stories,** but in **1926** she disappeared herself. She was found after a **10-day manhunt** and apparently had **no memory of what happened!**

# DISAPPEARANCES

An **Inuit settlement** in **Canada** was found abandoned in **1930.** A **Fire** was **alight** and all **personal belongings remained,** but the **30 residents were gone!**

# Old Angleland

**England from the 5th-century — AD 1066**

ANGLES and SAXONS were the main Anglo-Saxon tribes. The name 'ENGLAND' comes from 'Angle Land'.

Egbert, Ethelwulf, Ethelbald, 'Edward the Elder', Eadwig and 'Ethelred the Unready' were Anglo-Saxon Kings— England's **first monarchs!**

'LEECHES' were Anglo-Saxon **healers** who used **herbs, chants,** and **lucky charms** believed to make ill people **feel better.**

## Totally WEIRD!

**Invisible elves** were often **blamed** by Anglo-Saxons for **causing** any **pains** or **illnesses.**

The **STAFFORDSHIRE HOARD** is a trove of over **3,500 gold**, **silver** and **garnet treasures** that was **buried underground** by the Anglo-Saxons!

The Anglo Saxons **named** our **days of the week** after things like **gods**, **stars** and **planets.**

**MONDAY** = **Moon's** day
**TUESDAY** = **Tiw's** day (KING OF THE GODS)
**WEDNESDAY** = **Woden's** day (GOD OF WISDOM)
**THURSDAY** = **Thunor's** day (GOD OF THUNDER)
**FRIDAY** = **Frige's** day (GODDESS OF LOVE)
**SATURDAY** = **Saturn's** day
**SUNDAY** = **Sun's** day

Anglo-Saxons were
**VERY RESOURCEFUL.**
They used **animal fat** in **oil lamps**,
made **glue** from **cow bones**,
and used **deer antlers** as
**knife handles.**

# Incredible
# CREATURES

# CHAPTER 3

ZEBRAS live in large groups, called **HERDS.** As they move to new feeding grounds, **'SUPER HERDS'** may form consisting of **THOUSANDS** of individuals. They may team up with other **GRAZERS** on their travels, too, such as **ANTELOPES** and **WILDEBEEST.**

**Trot on to page 59 for more fantastic zebra facts.**

# COLOURFUL CRITTERS

Sometimes, nature is the best artist. Take a look at some of these radiant rainbow beasts!

**PEACOCK SPIDERS** are super small, growing no larger than 7 mm. But what they lack in size, they make up for in their flashy display of colours!

**MANDRILLS** are the largest of all monkeys. With patches of bright red and blue skin on their noses (and bottoms!) they are one of the most colourful mammal in the world.

**PANTHER CHAMELEONS** are an eye-catching species of lizard known for their rapid colour-changing abilities. Some males can completely change colour to match their surroundings in just 2 minutes!

**MANDARIN DUCKS** are known as the most beautiful ducks in the world thanks to their array of vibrant colours.

**LILAC-BREASTED ROLLERS** are brilliantly coloured birds living in Eastern and Southern Africa. The 'Roller' family of birds get their name from the impressive flight stunts they perform, like dives, swoops and rolls.

45

# LIVING on the EDGE

**VON DER DECKEN'S SIFAKAS** are lemurs that live in Madagascar's Tsingy de Bemaraha National Park.

As you can see, this isn't the kind of national park you could easily take a stroll through! The whole area is a fortress of razor-sharp limestone towers, some of which are over **760 metres** (2,500 feet) tall!

These ghostly looking lemurs leap from one rock formation to the next with ease, searching the park for food. The **thick** and **spongy pads** on their hands and feet, as well as their special way of jumping, are **amazing adaptations** that allow them to glide through the air and land lightly, never injuring themselves despite their harsh surroundings.

As well as moving effortlessly through the rocky Tsingy, **sifaka lemurs** can also live in mangroves and spiky thorn forests too!

Tsingy de Bemaraha National Park

## Totally **WEIRD!**

The name **'TSINGY'** comes from a word in the **Malagasy** language that means 'where one cannot walk barefoot'. Even though **humans struggle** to explore this 'forest' of serrated **needles,** Decken's sifakas don't seem to have a problem at all!

# MAD
# HAIR DAY

**GOOD, BAD OR MAD, THESE CRAZY CREATURES HAVE A HILARIOUS HAIR DAY, EVERY DAY!**

**KOMONDORS** are also known as 'mop dogs'… can you guess why!? They may look cuddly, but these brave dogs protect flocks of sheep from predators such as wolves.

**BUFF LACED POLISH** are a rare breed of chicken best known for their crazy crests that are also referred to as their 'top hat' feathers!

## MANGALICAS

are a Hungarian breed of big pig that grow thick, curly coats just like a sheep's wool! The name 'Mangalica' means 'hog with a lot of lard'.

## MACARONI PENGUINS

get their name from their funky yellow feathered crests, which look just like the 'macaroni feathers' that men of the 18th century wore in their hats!

## FRILLBACKS

are descendants of common rock dove pigeons that have been selectively bred to make their feathers as curly as possible!

## HOOPOES are funny-looking birds known for their distinctive crowns of feathers, which lie flat normally but rise and fan out when the birds get excited or alarmed!

# Magnificent
# MANDIBLES

Check out the
**MYSTERIOUS MOUTHPARTS**
of these **COOL CREATURES.**

**(But PLEASE don't
invite them to dinner!)**

## ORANGE NECTAR BATS

have a **tongue** with
a **special pumping
mechanism** that allows
them to **suck up nectar**
against the force of
**gravity.**

## MORAY EELS

have **two sets of jaws!**
First, they bite their
prey with the **'normal'
mouth jaws,** then,
**another set of jaws**
comes forward **from
their throat** to grip the
prey and **swallow it!**

## PLATYPUSES

are one of the **only mammals** to have a **flat bill** like a **duck's beak** and to hunt using 'electrolocation'. Their bill is so **sensitive** that it can **detect** the **electric fields** generated by **all living things!**

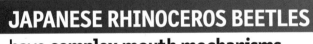

## JAPANESE RHINOCEROS BEETLES

have **complex mouth mechanisms** to help them chew. Their **interlocking mandibles** move together just **like the gearbox** of a car.

Did insects **invent gears** millions of years before us!?

## Totally **WEIRD!**

**Promachoteuthis sulcus** are **deep sea squids** with **lips** that cover their **beaks** and look just like **human teeth.**

51

# Creatures of the NIGHT

## 9 marvellous moth facts

**ATLAS MOTHS** can reach up to **30 centimetres** (12 inches) in **wingspan**. They're the **largest** moths in the **WORLD!**

**PLANTS** like **jasmine, honeysuckle** and evening **primrose** rely on moths for **pollination.** They give off strong, **perfumed scents** at night to attract them!

**NEPTICULIDAE,** or **'midget moths'**, are some of the **smallest** moths in the world, with **wingspans** of only **2.5 millimetres** (0.1 inches!).

52

Moths evolved to use the **moon** to **navigate** at night before **artificial light** was **invented.**

Which would **explain** why they're so **confused** by **light bulbs!**

**ROSY MAPLE MOTHS** are **beautiful pink** and **yellow** moths with extremely **woolly bodies!**

**MADAGASCAN MOON MOTHS,** also known as **comet moths,** are known for their **long 'tails'.**

There are around **160,000 species of moth** in the world (and only **17,500 species of butterfly!**).

**VAMPIRE MOTHS** are moths that have **evolved** from **piercing fruit** and **sucking nectar,** to **piercing skin** and **sucking blood!**

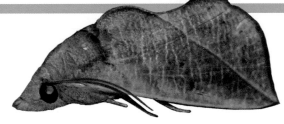

**HUMMINGBIRD HAWK MOTHS** use their **tongue-like proboscises** to collect **nectar** deep inside flowers.

# Wibble Wobble Jelly in the Sea

You might be surprised to find out just how many kinds of jelly-like creatures are lurking about in the depths of our oceans!

**LION'S MANE JELLYFISH,** or 'giant jellyfish', are the largest jellyfish in the world. With over 800 tentacles, they can measure up to 36 metres (120 feet) long – that's longer than a blue whale!

**MOON JELLYFISH** are harmless individually, but they can cause havoc in swarms. Sweden's biggest nuclear reactor once had to be shut down after a swarm of these jellyfish swam into the cooling outlet!

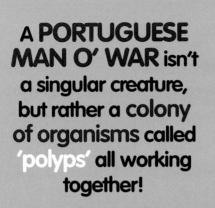

A **PORTUGUESE MAN O' WAR** isn't a singular creature, but rather a colony of organisms called 'polyps' all working together!

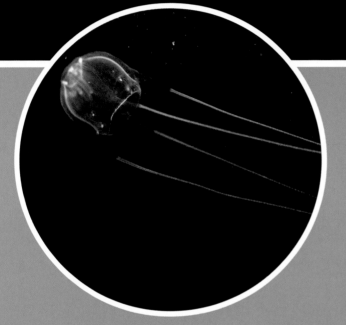

**IRUKANDJI JELLYFISH** are the smallest and most venomous jellyfish in the world. They are transparent and usually only the size of a thumbnail... good luck trying to avoid these tiny menaces!

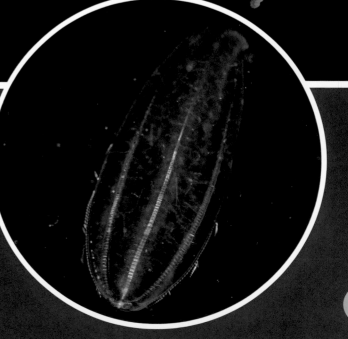

**CTENOPHORES** are fascinating marine creatures that give off rainbow coloured pulses as they move through the water. They also go by many other funny names, including 'comb jellies', 'sea gooseberries', and 'sea walnuts'!

# Take a tour of TOKYO'S CREATURE CAFES

Visiting a nice cafe couldn't get any better, unless... that cafe was full of your favourite animals! Tokyo has truly embraced creature cafe culture – which one of these amazing animal cafes would you visit?

**Cat cafes,** where cat-loving cafe-goers can **play with kitties** during their visit, first started in **Japan in 2004.**
Since then, the trend for all kinds of **animal cafes** has grown.

**DID YOU KNOW?**
There are over 150 cat cafes in Japan!

## PIG CAFES

Here, visitors can enjoy the company of the **cutest** things on **four trotters: micro pigs!** Unlike regular pigs, which can grow to become 300 kilograms (47 stone), the **little pigs** at this cafe only grow to around **60 kilograms (9 stone).**

## HEDGEHOG CAFES

Hedgehog cafes are becoming more and more **popular** in **Japan.** You'll need to wear **special gloves** to have afternoon tea with these **spiky friends!**

## SNAKE CAFES

Don't worry, these cafes aren't as **scary** as they sound! All the **snakes** are **non-venomous** and you can even **eat snake-themed food!** Snake cakes, anyone?

## REPTILE CAFES

Reptile cafes are **perfect** for **lizard lovers.** Some have over **100 creatures** to hang out with. Iced tea and **iguanas** sounds like a perfect combination.

# EARNING THEIR STRIPES

These ANIMALS have earned their place in the HALL OF FASHION FAME thanks to their STYLISH STRIPES!

## INDIAN PALM SQUIRRELS

are **small rodents** found in **India.** They have **three distinctive stripes** across their backs. They are **considered sacred** by some people!

**NUMBATS** are **small marsupials** native to **Australia.** They have long **sticky tongues** to help them pick up **termites,** and they're also known as '**banded anteaters.**'

**ZEBRAS** may all look the same to us, but each of them has a **completely unique pattern of stripes.** One **theory** for these **super-stripes** is that they help **regulate temperature.**

**OKAPIS** are native to the **Democratic Republic of the Congo** in Central Africa. Their striped markings may look like those of a **zebra**, but okapis are actually **more closely related to giraffes!**

**RING-TAILED LEMURS** can have seriously **stinky tails!** These cheeky creatures like to **rub smelly secretions** into their tails and give a **whiffy wave** to their **rivals.**

59

# WORLD'S UGLIEST dogs

These **dogs** don't mind their **ugliness**, they **embrace it** – and **win prizes** for it too! For over **30 years**, the annual **World's Ugliest Dog Contest** has been celebrating the **beauty** in the **lovable imperfections** of some **crazy canine** characters.

## LET'S MEET THE CHAMPIONS...

ZSA ZSA

A **droopy-tongued English bulldog** named **Zsa Zsa** scooped the award in 2018. Her **wide stance** and **unmistakable underbite** helped see off her **competitors.**

## SCAMP THE TRAMP

Now **'SCAMP THE CHAMP'**, this **little pooch** owes his 2019 success to his **bug-eyes** and **matted grey fur** that cannot be tamed, no matter how many trips he takes to the **dog groomers!**

Scamp used to be a **stray dog,** until his owner Yvonne adopted him. On their way home from the rescue centre Scamp was **so happy** he **bobbed** his head, in time, to **reggae music.** Since adoption, he has been bringing **joy** wherever he goes in his job as a **pet therapist.** He loves to **visit senior citizens** and school children and make them **smile,** and he's even a **loving 'uncle'** to several **foster kittens!**

## MARTHA

**Martha** is a **huge mastiff dog** that was crowned the World's Ugliest Dog back in 2017. She won the competition thanks to her **droopy jowls,** and **bossy personality!**

61

# Meet the BEASTS of BORNEO

BORNEO IS ONE OF THE MOST BIODIVERSE PLACES IN THE WORLD! HERE, YOU'LL DISCOVER PLENTY OF CURIOUS CREATURES...

**CHEVROTAINS** are also known as **'mouse deer'**, but they aren't mice or deer! The **smallest hoofed mammals** in the world, these cuties are only the **size of cats!**

**SUN BEARS** might just be the **strangest-looking bears** in the world! According to **folklore**, the **yellow shape** in their **chest fur** is thought, by some, to resemble the **rising sun!**

## BORNEO PYGMY ELEPHANTS
are the **world's smallest elephants,** growing to around **2.5 metres** (7 feet) tall. In comparison, **African elephants** can grow up to **4 metres** (13 feet) in height!

## BORNEAN SLOW LORIS
**weigh less** than the average **guinea pig!** These **tiny animals** have **huge eyes** containing a **reflective layer** that helps them **see at night.**

## PROBOSCIS MONKEYS
are **famous** for their **nose.** The **male** has an **unusually long** and **bulbous nose,** which can **grow** to over **10 centimetres** (4 inches) in length!

## CLOUDED LEOPARDS
are **mysterious,** and very **rarely spotted!** Their name is thought to come from the **blotchy 'clouds'** of their spot pattern.

# Bright
# IDEAS

**FOLDABLE** mobile phones aren't just physically **FLEXIBLE.** Having two parts to the screen means that the user can do **TWO THINGS** at the **SAME TIME.** Want to watch a video **AND** talk to a friend at the same time? Maybe a foldable phone is the way **FORWARD.**

10:32

**Flip to page 70 for more marvellous mobiles.**

# CHAPTER 4

Ketuk untuk info cuaca
Google
Play Store
Galeri
Galaxy Store

# SINGAPORE'S

# SUPERTREES

**SUPERTREES are the STARS of the SHOW at GARDENS BY THE BAY in SINGAPORE!**

A man-made, mechanical forest of 18 of these giant trees tower over the city's gardens, ranging from 25 metres (82 feet) to 50 metres (164 feet) in height – that's as tall as a 16-storey building!

But what are supertrees and why are they such cool inventions? These high-tech structures have cores of reinforced concrete to hold them upright. Their trunks are made from steel frames, with a layer of 'living skin' over the top, which includes more than 150,000 live plants across the gardens!

As well as being fascinating vertical gardens that put on awesome displays of colourful lights and music each evening, the supertrees are also doing lots of amazing things for the environment. Some of the supertrees have 'photovoltaic' cells that harvest the sun's light and convert it into energy. Other supertrees act as air vents and exhausts for the garden's conservatories, as well as collecting rainwater, absorbing heat, and moderating temperature. These robot trees really do it all!

## Totally **WEIRD!**

And as if that wasn't **cool** enough, one of the **supertrees** also has a **50-metre-high bistro** (164 feet), and you can travel along a huge **'Skyway'** walk from one supertree to another!

# The SCOOP on SCOPES

**ELECTRON MICROSCOPES** can make images that are half an atom wide. With great power, comes a great price tag, with the most expensive electron microscope costing over £20 million.

The **JAMES WEBB SPACE TELESCOPE** is the world's most expensive telescope, costing around £8 billion to make over 20 years!

**PERISCOPES** are used to look at things from hidden positions (like looking at the surface from an underwater submarine!).

The **GRAN TELESCOPIO CANARIAS** is the biggest single aperture telescope in the world, measuring 10.4 metres (34 feet) wide.

## Totally **WEIRD!**

A **photo** of a honey **bee's eye** covered in **pollen** won a **microscopic photography competition!**

The **HUBBLE TELESCOPE** has made more than 1.3 million observations about our universe!

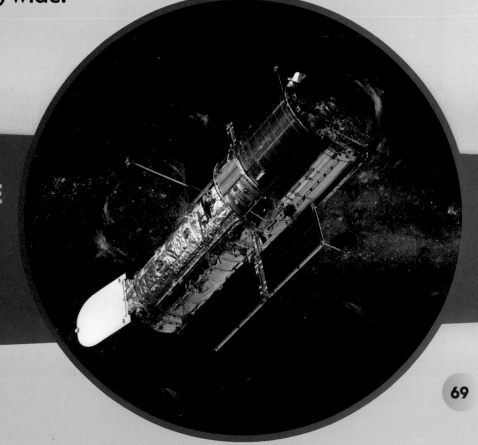

# 145 years of
## funky PHONES

2021 is the 145th anniversary of the telephone being invented! Phones have transformed in many interesting ways since Alexander Graham Bell invented them back in 1876...

The first 'smartphone' was invented in 1992, nearly 30 years ago! It could make calls, receive emails, and send faxes. It was revolutionary at the time.

'Ahoy!' was the original greeting Alexander Graham Bell suggested should be used when making telephone calls, until Thomas Edison suggested using 'hello' instead! Which do you prefer?

The Mobile Phone Throwing World Championships have been held in Finland for over 20 years! The current record for throwing a mobile phone stands at over 110 metres (360 feet)! Unbelievable!

Snake was one of the first games to be played on mobile phones. Since it began in 1997, it has been played on around 400 million phones worldwide!

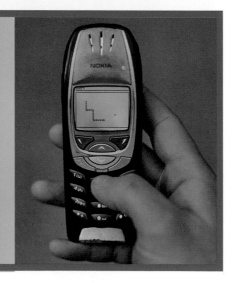

Mobile phones are dirtier than toilets! According to some studies, around 18 times more bacteria can be found on a phone screen than on a toilet flush handle.

The world's first foldable phone was released in 2019. Will all phones be flexible one day? Who knows! We'll just have to see how the future unfolds...

## DID YOU KNOW?

666 6666 is the world's most expensive phone number. It sold in a charity auction in Qatar for around £1.5 million!

# The perfect
# PICK-ME-UP

The **GUARDIAN XO** is one of the coolest robots around! It is a heavy-duty suit, or to use its fancier name, 'a powered exoskeleton', that gives the wearer super-strength! It helps pick up almost anything!

It was designed to help warehouse workers by making them 20 times stronger! That means things feel 20 times lighter if you are using the robot suit. It can help people lift 90 kilograms (200 pounds).

The robot suit is also a great way to prevent injuries and maximise the physical potential of humans.

**WHAT WOULD YOU USE ONE FOR?**

The SUIT TRANSFORMS whoever wears it into a mega-cool robot-cyborg who can lift things they never could have before!

It is also one of the most efficient robot devices around because it does not use too much energy.

73

# Spine-shocking

**EPIDURAL ELECTRICAL STIMULATORS** are **high-tech implants** that **help paralysed people to walk** again by using **electric shocks!** These **tiny implants** are attached to people's **spinal cords,** transmitting **electrical signals** along their **spine.** Some people who thought they may **never be able to walk again** can **now walk** thanks to these **super helpful gadgets!**

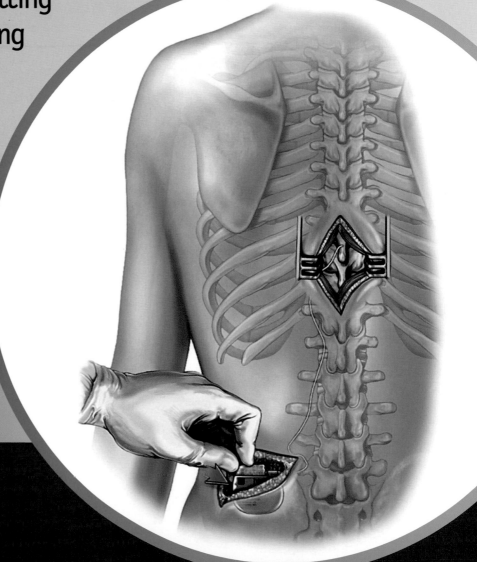

**Placement of stimulator**

# RECOVERIES...

**Stimulator with morphine pump to help with pain**

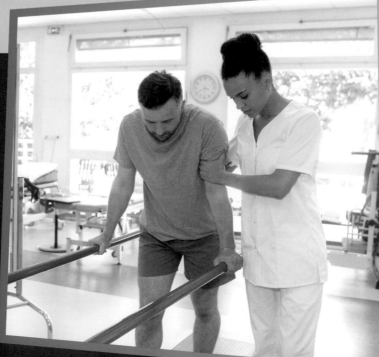

Even when they are **not moving,** this amazing implant is **activating feelings** and **repairing parts of the person's nervous system** that had seemed **lost.** What's even **more exciting** about this, is that the implants were **first designed just to treat pain!** The fact that they **helped paralysed people to start moving** again was a **very happy accident!**

**DID YOU KNOW?**

One patient was able to walk 100 metres with a walking frame on the day the implant was fitted.

# extraordinary
## Eco-inventions

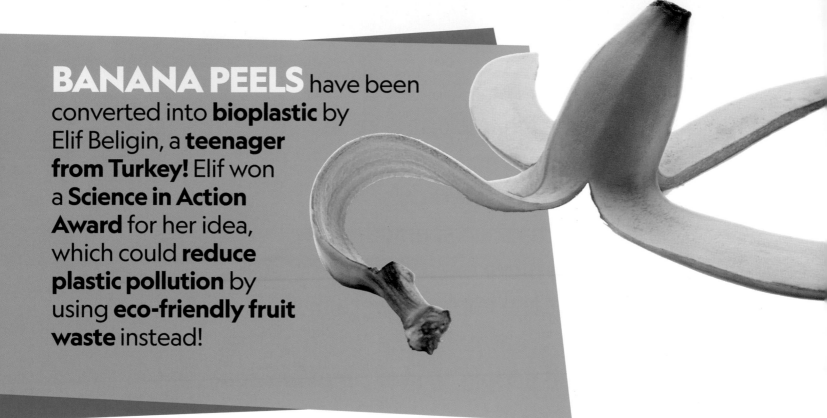

**BANANA PEELS** have been converted into **bioplastic** by Elif Beligin, a **teenager from Turkey!** Elif won a **Science in Action Award** for her idea, which could **reduce plastic pollution** by using **eco-friendly fruit waste** instead!

**EDIBLE WATER BLOBS** could one day **replace plastic water bottles!** These **water spheres** are made from **edible algae gel** that's completely **biodegradable!**

**LEFTOVER COFFEE** and **TEA WASTE** could be **recycled** and used **instead of ink** thanks to a new **eco-friendly printer.**

**WORM HIVES** are **boxes of meal-worms** that can be fed with any **leftovers,** which **reduces food waste** and **creates natural fertiliser.** (You can also **eat the worms** for **protein** if you're **brave enough!**)

77

# Lean, MEAN, CLEANING MACHINES

Check out these weird new gadgets that might be helping us clean up in the future.

**VOICE-ACTIVATED TAPS** can dispense water on command. Users can tell these taps exactly how much water to dispense and can ask for a specific temperature too!

**SMART TECH BINS** have bin bags that seal themselves once the bin is full, then automatically get replaced once the bin bag is removed!

# Totally **WEIRD!**

A clothing company have created baby clothes that double up as floor polishers so little ones clean as they crawl. Hilarious but probably not very hygienic!

## SMART LITTER BOXES

are one of the latest futuristic gadgets to help kitty owners with their tasks. These artificially intelligent cat toilets gather data about pets' pooping habits so they can self-clean right on time!

**Y-BRUSH** is a wacky y-shaped sonic toothbrush with 96 bristle clusters that can apparently clean half your mouth in just 10 seconds!

# Mindboggling
# BUILDINGS

**THE BIG DUCK** on Long Island in New York was built by a duck farmer, **MARTIN MAURER,** in 1931. It is the main building on **BIG DUCK RANCH,** which, in 2008, was added to the **NATIONAL REGISTER OF HISTORIC PLACES.**

# CHAPTER 5

**Fly over to page 88 for more buildings in disguise.**

# Cyber CHAPEL

# TORRE GIRONA

in Barcelona, Spain, may look like a normal chapel from the outside but step inside and you'll discover it's anything but normal! This unsuspicious-looking building is home to one of the most interesting supercomputers in the world: **THE MARENOSTRUM.**

Inside the old architecture of the Torre Girona you'll find ultramodern glass and steel encasing the MareNostrum — the most powerful supercomputer in Spain! The main computer block is made up of 165,888 processors and a whopping memory of 390 terabytes (390,000 gigabytes!). At its peak power, this supercomputer can perform more than eleven thousand trillion operations per second!

Who would've thought that an old chapel building could be home to an awesome supercomputer used for weather forecasting, astrophysical simulations, climate change projects, and even human genome research!?

# SURPRISING stays

Who would want to stay in a normal hotel when extraordinary places like these exist!?

## PALACIO DE SAL, BOLIVIA

This hotel is built on the **largest salt flat in the world.** And guess what? The **entire hotel** is made of **salt blocks.**

## MAGIC MOUNTAIN, CHILE

This **volcano-shaped** hotel has its own **waterfall** and the **entrance** is a **hanging bridge.**

**Fancy staying overnight inside a zoo?** Give this place a try. You can **sleep in front** of animals like **lemurs, polar bears,** or **tigers** – if you're brave enough...

## The surprises don't end there! Exciting hotels aren't just for people...

### Totally **WEIRD!**

**Marmara Antalya, Turkey,** has the only **rotating** hotel building in the world. It turns **360°** so the **view** from each room is constantly **changing!**

**PATCH PLANT HOTEL, ENGLAND,** is the **world's first hotel for plants.** 'Plant parents' can describe their **plant's 'personality'** when checking-in to ensure their plants are well looked after.

**CATZONIA, MALAYSIA,** is the **world's first five-star hotel for cats.** VVIC (Very Very Important Cat) rooms come with three beds, a **mini playground** and wi-fi. And, if cats want to **really indulge** they can get **pampered** at **resort's spa.**

85

# A postman's
# PALACE

**LE PALAIS IDÉAL** (the 'Ideal Palace') in Hauterives, France is a weird and wonderful building constructed by the French postman **Ferdinand Cheval.** Cheval had no training in building and knew nothing about architecture, but he **built the palace entirely by himself!**

Every day during his work as a postman, Cheval would **collect stones** and **rocks.** Once he got back to his home, he would work each night by the light of an **oil lamp** to put them all together using **lime, cement** and mortar.

The whole process took **33 years!** By the time Cheval finished creating his palace, he was something of an **expert!**

The palace itself is a curious combination of **architectural styles** from around the world: the **south side** of the building looks like a cross between Angkor Wat and **La Sagrada Familia** (even though Cheval had never visited them!), **the east side** of the building looks like an Egyptian temple (and includes two waterfalls!), and the **north side** of the building has upper walls lined with carvings of animals, including ostriches, **octopi, lions,** flamingos, **dragons,** a polar bear and a **1.2-metre** (4-foot) camel!

Cheval carved **quotes** and **poems** all over the palace, including this most famous one:

'1879–1912 10,000 days, 93,000 hours, 33 years of struggle. Let those who think they can do better try.'

# Buildings in DISGUISE

The **HIGH HEEL WEDDING CHURCH** in **Taiwan** is definitely one of the most **stylish buildings** in the world!

The **BASKET BUILDING** in **Ohio, USA,** was once the **headquarters** of a company that made... you guessed it! **BASKETS!**

The **BIG DUCK** in **New York, USA,** is a **souvenir shop** selling all things duck-related.

The **ELEPHANT TOWER** in **Bangok, Thailand,** is supposed to look like an elephant... **Can you spot the tusks?**

This **former petrol** station in **Washington State, USA,** is shaped like a **GIANT TEAPOT!**

The **SNAIL HOUSE** in **Sofia, Bulgaria,** is a **colourful mega mollusc** with **five floors** and **no straight walls!**

# Seven
## of the oldest

The **ĠGANTIJA TEMPLES** in Malta are two of the world's oldest religious buildings. According to local folklore, they were built by a giantess who ate nothing but broad beans and honey!

**TUMULUS OF BOUGON** is a group of five Neolithic 'barrows' (burial mounds) built in France in 4700 BC – that's around 2,000 years before the Egyptian pyramids were built!

**AL-QARAWIYYIN LIBRARY** in Morocco opened in the year AD 859, making it the oldest library in the world. When it was restored, a secret, hidden manuscript room was discovered!

**HŌRYŪ-JI** in Japan is the oldest wooden building in the world! Built around AD 700, the wooden temple has been standing for over 1,300 years!

**KNAP OF HOWAR** in Scotland are two of the oldest preserved stone houses in the world. People lived there from 3700 BC to 2800 BC!

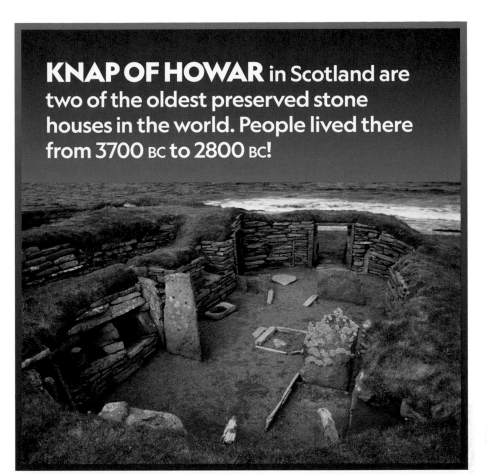

The **AMPHITHEATRE OF POMPEII** is the oldest surviving Roman amphitheatre in the world. In AD 79, it was buried by the volcanic eruption of nearby Vesuvius.

# BENEATH the SURFACE

Forget skyscrapers towering high above the ground... get to know these underground buildings buried beneath!

**WIELICZKA SALT MINE** in **Poland** was one of the **WORLD'S OLDEST** salt mines, operating for over **700 YEARS** – until it transformed into an **UNDERGROUND MUSEUM, ART GALLERY** and **CHAPEL!**

## Totally **WEIRD!**

The **chapel** at Wieliczka Salt Mine was **carved** out of salt by **miners.** Better still, it has a carving of Leonardo da Vinci's **'The Last Supper'.**

## GJØVIK OLYMPIC CAVERN HALL

Gjøvik Olympic Cavern Hall in Norway is the world's largest underground auditorium. Buried 120 metres (390 feet) into a mountain, this hall includes an ice hockey rink, a swimming pool, and space for over 5,000 people!

## SHELL GROTTO

Shell Grotto in England is an underground passageway and chamber covered in over 4 million seashells! This mysterious place was discovered in 1835, but no one knows when (or why) it was built!

## TEMPPELIAUKIO CHURCH

Temppeliaukio Church in Finland, also known as the Rock Church, was built directly into solid rock! Light is let in through skylights that surround the huge domed ceiling.

## TURF HOUSES

Turf houses in Iceland are insulated by layers of grass that surround the walls and even grow on top of the roof!

# The FUTURE is GREEN

**Only some of these modern buildings are green in colour, but all of them are eco-friendly!**

Wat Pa Maha Chedi Kaew in Sisaket, Thailand, is made from over 1.5 million recycled beer bottles! It's also known as the 'Temple of a Million Bottles'!

The Bahrain World Trade Center is the first skyscraper in the world to include wind turbines as part of it's architectural design!

The **largest vertical gardens** in the world cover an apartment building in **Columbia.** Over **100,000 plants** grow on the building, **cleaning enough air** for around **700 people** by filtering **harmful gases!**

Bosco Verticale (vertical forest) in Milan, Italy, are a pair of residential towers standing 112 metres (367 feet) and 76 metres (249 feet) tall. They are home to more than 800 trees.

**Pixel Building in Australia** isn't just funky, it's also completely self-sustaining! It collects all of its own water and generates electricity through renewable energy!

Coconut School in Phnom Penh, Cambodia is built almost entirely from rubbish like tyres, plastic cups, and bottles. It offers free tuition in English and computer literacy as well as teaching students about respecting the environment.

# WOOD you BELIEVE it?

## LET'S EXPLORE SOME TERRIFIC TREETOP STRUCTURES

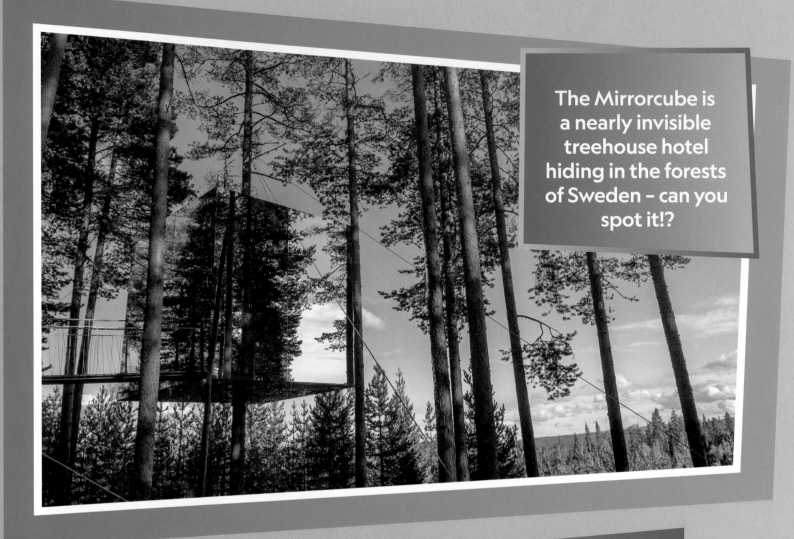

The Mirrorcube is a nearly invisible treehouse hotel hiding in the forests of Sweden – can you spot it!?

Teahouse Tetsu is a Japanese teahouse built among cherry blossom trees.

# Totally **WEIRD!**

In **Thailand,** some fancy resorts have their very own **tree-top swimming pool!**

**These Treehouse Lodges in Peru are perched up high with the monkeys, sloths, and birds of the Amazon rainforest!**

These 'glamping' treehouses in Canada are perfectly spherical.

**Steampunk Treehouse is a bizarre angular treehouse art installation built around a 12-metre (40-feet) metal tree!**

97

# Get a
## MOVE ON!

# CHAPTER 6

In **SOAPBOX RACING COMPETITIONS** teams are **JUDGED** on the **TIME** it takes them to complete the **COURSE** as well as the **DESIGN** of their **CAR.**

Zoom to page 114 for more on soapbox cars.

# Right on TRACK...

The **MAEKLONG RAILWAY MARKET** near Bangkok is similar to other markets in Thailand – it's **colourful**, bustling, and a great place to buy **fresh fruit** and **vegetables.** But there's one crazy thing that makes this market in particular completely unique: **train tracks pass right through the middle of it!**

Up to **eight times per day,** a train runs through the market, **blowing its horn** and **transforming** the entire place as it goes along. Sellers and **stall owners** have to **quickly** and calmly move all of their baskets and **umbrellas off the tracks** and draw their overhead shades back to get out of the train's way!

It's a **narrow squeeze,** with the train driving **so close** by that it actually passes directly over some of the **food baskets on the tracks.** Market sellers are completely used to this weird occurrence as it's just **part of everyday life** for them, but train drivers have to watch out for **tourists,** who often get **dangerously close** to the tracks to try to snap a great photo!

# RECORD-BREAKING motors

The **Bugatti Chiron Super Sport** is the **FASTEST CAR IN THE WORLD.** It can reach speeds of **304 miles per hour** (490 kilometres per hour).

After retirement, **space shuttle Endeavour** was **driven** to **California Science Centre** through the streets of **Los Angeles.** It is **23 metres** (75 feet) **wide** (6 lanes) and **37 metres** (121 feet) long.

The modified **Lamborghini Murcielago** is one of the **loudest vehicles** in the world. Measuring in at **142 decibels**, it is *louder* than a **passenger jet taking off!**

**Minings trucks** are the **tallest vehicles in the world.** Some measure over **8 metres** (26 feet) **tall** and are **SO BIG** that they *cannot* be **driven on the roads.**

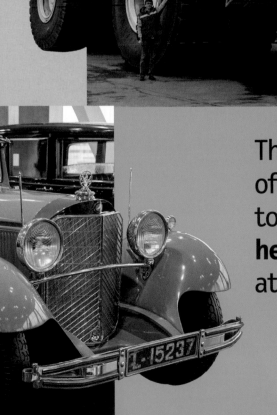

The **Mercedes Benz 770** is one of the **HEAVIEST CARS EVER** to be made. It really is one **hefty motor,** weighing in at nearly

**5 tonnes!**

# the COOLEST
# AIRPORT in the WORLD

**CHANGI AIRPORT** in **Singapore** is one of Asia's busiest, not to mention, one of the most interesting!

It is the **only airport** in the world with a butterfly garden. It also features an impressive rain sculpture called **'kinetic rain'** that has to be seen to be believed!

Have you ever been to an airport with an entertainment deck, a cinema, a rooftop **cactus garden**, an orchid garden with a **koi fish pond**, a swimming pool, and a **jacuzzi** too!? Changi has it all!

And, as if that wasn't enough, the airport is also home to loads of other cool things like the world's only indoor circular waterfall, the **biggest slide** in any airport (and the highest slide in Singapore), and a giant 'social tree' that's nearly **9 metres** (29 feet) tall and covered in **64 screens** where airport visitors can share their photos and videos!

GIANT SLIDES

CACTUS GARDEN

CHANGI
airport singapore

@ChangiAirport

BUTTERFLY GARDEN

SOCIAL TREE

INDOOR WATERFALL

MOVIE THEATRE

KINETIC RAIN

**Jungfraujoch Station** in **Switzerland** is **Europe's highest train station!** At 3,454 metres (11,322 feet) above sea level, there's plenty to take in from this view!

# DESTINATION stations

## These train stations are impressive destinations in themselves!

**Atocha Station** in **Spain** is one of the most **tropical** you will see! It's like a **jungle** in there. A 4,000 square metre (43,000 square foot) tropical garden makes waiting for the train an **adventure** in itself!

**Chhatrapati Shivaji Terminus** in **India** is over **130 years old**. Known for its impressive **architecture** and **history,** it is one of Mumbai's **UNESCO** World Heritage Sites!

**São Bento Station** in **Portugal** is known for its floor-to-ceiling tile **artwork.** There are over **20,000 tiles** that tell the **story** of Portugal's past.

## DID YOU KNOW?

Grand Central Station in New York has 44 platforms, the most platforms of any station in the world!

# Canine CROSSING

**TOKYO'S SHIBUYA CROSSING** IS THE **BUSIEST PEDESTRIAN CROSSING** IN THE WORLD!

People are allowed to cross on **two minute cycles** (meaning that two minutes of **absolute chaos** is followed by two minutes of **calm!)**

Many **tourists visit** the crossing just to **stand and watch** the **spectacle** of so many masses of people crossing! At **peak times,** there are literally **thousands** of people **dodging each other** which is why this **crazy intersection** has earned the nickname '**the scramble'**.

You'll also find a **bronze statue** of a **dog** named **HACHIKO** near the crossing, who used to visit Shibuya Station every day. Hachiko has become an unofficial **landmark of Japan**, with many people now referring to Shibuya Crossing as **Hachiko Crossing** instead! The statue's **legs are polished** because so many people passing by have **petted him.** He may not play fetch but he is very good at sitting.

# Extraordinary
## elevators

## BURJ KHALIFA ELEVATOR

The Burj Khalifa elevator, Dubai, is one of the fastest elevators in the world, reaching speeds of up to 64 kilometres per hour (40 miles per hour)!

## STREPY-THIEU BOAT LIFT

The Strepy-Thieu Boat lift, Belgium, is the beefiest of its kind. It can lift up to 8,400 tonnes!

## THE SHIPLIFT

The shiplift at Three Gorges Dam, China, is the world's biggest ship elevator (it's as tall as a 40-storey building!)

## SANTA JUSTA LIFT

The Santa Justa Lift, Portugal, is a national monument famous for its unique Neo-Gothic design.

## FALKIRK WHEEL

The Falkirk Wheel, Scotland, is the world's only rotating boat lift!

## AUTOSTADT SILOS

Autostadt Silos, Germany, are a pair of car towers where shuttles are used to lift and lower vehicles in preparation for distribution.

## AQUADOM

The AquaDom, Germany, is the world's only lift in an aquarium!

**The Taylor Aerocar** was designed to be the world's only practical flying car! Once this aircraft landed, it folded its wings away and drove right out of the airport!

**The Northrop Grumman B-2 Spirit** is a super-sneaky aircraft, with a slim, flat 'flying wing' design that's almost impossible to see from the side!

**DID YOU KNOW?**

Although used mainly for passengers, Concorde was used to transport diamonds and human organs.

**Concorde** was the fastest passenger plane in existence. It travelled at Mach 2 speed (2,180 kilometres per hour or 1,350 miles per hour) and could fly from London to New York in around three hours!

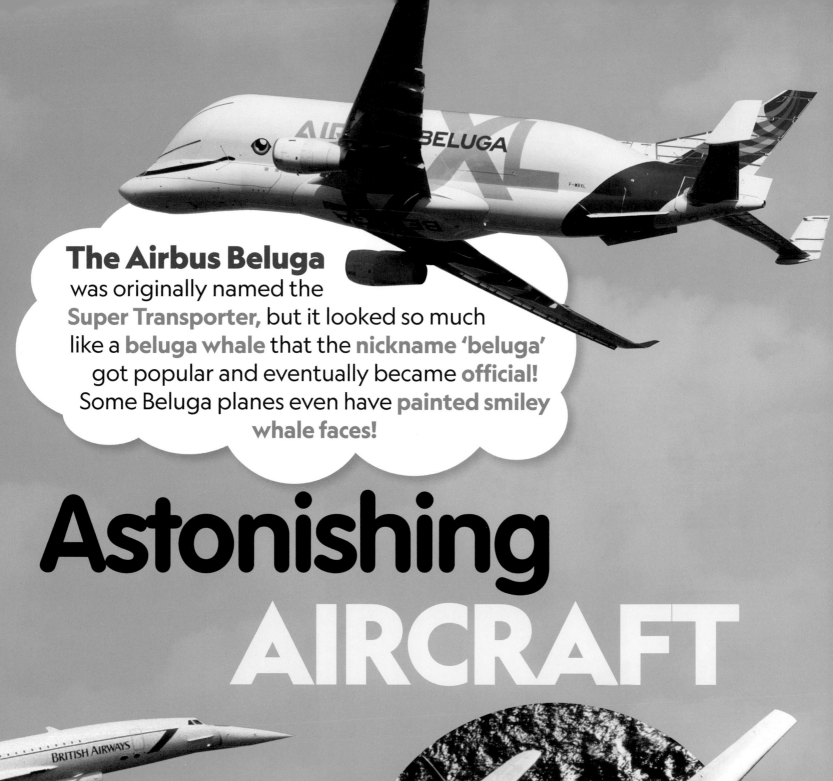

**The Airbus Beluga** was originally named the **Super Transporter,** but it looked so much like a **beluga whale** that the **nickname 'beluga'** got popular and eventually became **official!** Some Beluga planes even have **painted smiley whale faces!**

# Astonishing AIRCRAFT

**The H-4 Hercules seaplane,** also known as the **Spruce Goose,** was the **largest flying boat ever built,** with a **whopping wingspan** of **98 metres (320 feet)!**

# Good clean FUN

**SOAPBOX RACING** got its **name** because people originally used to **race** in cars built from **wooden soap crates** with **wheels attached to them!**

**SOAPBOX CARS** have **no engines!** They must be **powered by gravity** (but they're allowed a **good old-fashioned push** at the **start** of the **race!**).

LOTS OF DIFFERENT NAMES ARE GIVEN TO SOAPBOX CARS: LIKE 'BOGIES', 'CARTIES', OR 'PILERS' IN SCOTLAND AND ENGLAND, 'GAMBO' IN WALES AND 'BILLY CARTS' IN AUSTRALIA!

**SOAPBOX RACES** are famously fun! People race in **costumes** and **decorate** cars in **wacky themes.** Each race begins with a **dance routine,** and often includes **jumps** and **obstacles!**

**DID YOU KNOW?**

Formula 1 champion Sebastian Vettel famously gave soapbox racing a go! He had fun racing in full Super Mario costume, but he said he 'prefers motors'!

Bathtubs, burgers, sheep, spaceships, sandwiches, and even rolls of toilet paper are among some of the bizarre but brilliant things people have decorated their cars to look like!

115

# Out of this WORLD!

# CHAPTER 7

Approximately **ONCE A YEAR,** an **ASTEROID** the size of a **CAR** enters the **EARTH'S ATMOSPHERE.** Fortunately, it **BURNS UP** before it reaches the **SURFACE.**

**Drop in on page 129 for more about amazing asteroids.**

# TITAN...

## is this the Universe's stinkiest moon?

**TITAN IS THE LARGEST MOON OF SATURN.** Its atmosphere is super cold, the average surface temperature is around −179°C! Titan's atmosphere contains much more methane than Earth and it comes in the form as a solid, a liquid and a gas. Titan's methane cycle works much like Earth's water cycle, meaning that on this moon there are methane clouds, and even methane rain! Because liquid methane has a different surface tension to water, the raindrops would be around twice the size of the raindrops here on Earth, and they would fall super slowly thanks to Titan's weak gravity.

**SCIENTISTS** have noticed that Titan's oceans have **no waves.** They think that Titan is now entering a more **windy season** which may bring winds strong enough to form **waves** in the **thick liquid methane** the oceans are made of.

## Totally **WEIRD!**

**Methane** is the **main gas** in our **burps** and **trumps.** Imagine the **smell** of this place! But you would **never get the chance to smell** it because the **atmosphere is so cold** it would **freeze your nose right off!**

**LAB-GROWN MEAT** has been successfully made in space by taking **cells from a cow** to the International Space Station (ISS), then using a **3D bioprinter** to grow a Petri dish full of **muscle tissue!**

The **INTERNATIONAL SPACE STATION** **orbits** Earth every **90 minutes,** meaning it travels through **16 sunrises** and **sunsets** in just **24 hours.**

On board the **ISS**, there are **two bathrooms, six sleeping quarters,** and over **50 computers** to control the station's many systems! There's also a **gym** where astronauts have to do **exercise** for at least **two hours each day.**

# INTERNATIONAL ACE STATION

The International Space Station is **BIG!** It measures over **108 metres** (354 feet) long from one end to the other, and it **weighs** around the same as **320 cars!**

The International Space Station is the **MOST EXPENSIVE STRUCTURE EVER BUILT,** costing over **£100 billion** (and counting—the cost **continuously rises** while the station continues to operate!).

# CREATURES of the COSMOS

THERE ARE SO MANY GALAXIES OUT THERE IN THE VAST UNIVERSE, BUT WOULD YOU BELIEVE THAT SOME OF THEM ARE SHAPED JUST LIKE ANIMALS WE KNOW AND LOVE ON EARTH!?

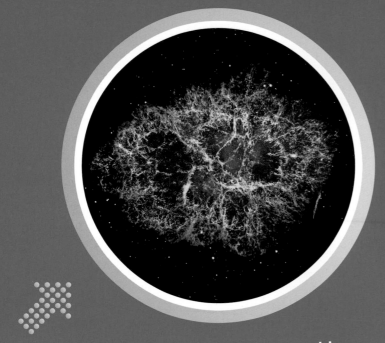

The **CRAB NEBULA** was formed by an **exploding star.** It shone so brightly it could be **seen from Earth with binoculars.**

The **EAGLE NEBULA** gets its name because it looks like a **bird in flight.**

The **HORSEHEAD NEBULA** is part of the **massive Orion nebula.**

The MICE GALAXIES have **long tails** that are formed by the **gravitational pulls** of nearby galaxies.

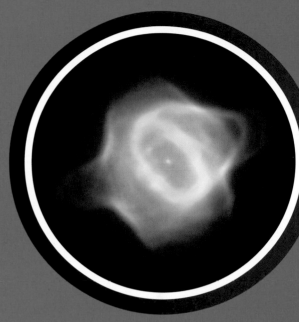

The **STINGRAY NEBULA** is the **youngest known nebula,** visible since early last century.

TADPOLE GALAXY gets its name from its long tail, which will **one day break off** to form a **smaller galaxy.**

The GIANT SQUID NEBULA looks like a **ghostly** giant squid **swimming** through the dark ocean of space!

# the quest for
# QUASARS

**QUASARS** are **POWERFUL BURSTS OF ENERGY** that are thought to **BLAST OUT OF BOTH ENDS OF SUPERMASSIVE BLACK HOLES** in the centre of **LARGE GALAXIES.**

Some quasars give off more energy than 600 trillion Suns!

Quasars are the most distant observable objects in the known Universe, they exist at the 'edges of the Universe' and are constantly moving away from us.

Quasars are so bright that they can shine through entire galaxies, they are some of the only known examples of objects bright enough to do this.

Quasars look like red flashes of light because their white light is being bent towards the red end of the light spectrum as they move away from Earth, this is called 'red shift.'

Quasars were first discovered in the 1950s when scientists picked up powerful radio waves but didn't know where they were coming from!

The farthest known quasar is 13 billion light years away from Earth! That is a very, very long way indeed.

# Bon voyage!

## THE EPIC JOURNEY OF VOYAGER 1

**VOYAGER 1** is a **spacecraft** that has been **travelling away from Earth for over 40 years!** It is currently the furthest man-made object from Earth in existence.

**Voyager 1 launch**

After its **launch in 1977**, Voyager 1 reached **Jupiter in 1979** and Saturn in 1980. This was made possible by an **alignment** of the **solar system's planets** that happens once every 176 years. **Voyager 1** used the **gravity** from each of the aligned planets to 'slingshot' into the next planet's orbit and **beyond!**

Voyager 1 was designed to communicate with intelligent life forms. Onboard, it carries disks called 'golden records' that are loaded up with examples of human culture such as music, photos, sounds, and phrases from Earth. If any other life forms do discover it one day, they'll find music by Mozart, whale sounds, and even a recording of a baby crying!

Over 38,000 years from now, in the year 40,272, Voyager 1 is expected to pass 'near' to a star that makes up part of the Ursa Minor constellation, also known as the 'Little Bear' which contains the group of stars known as the 'Little Dipper'.

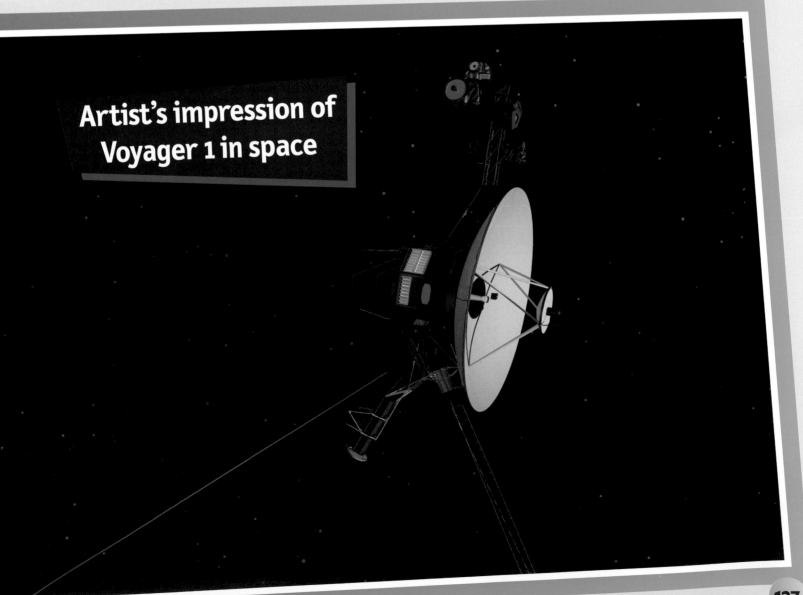

Artist's impression of Voyager 1 in space

# DIAMONDS in the SKY

**WHITE DWARFS** are **stars** that are about to die. Scientists think that as they **cool,** the **cores** of these stars may **crystallise** to form **giant diamonds!**

There is so much **GOLD** in an **asteroid** called **16 Psyche** that it could make everyone on **Earth** a **BILLIONAIRE!**

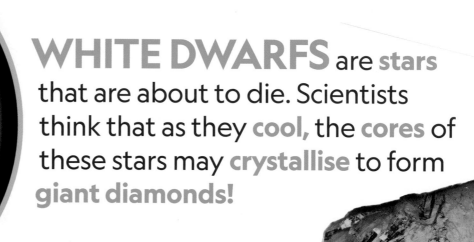

## DIAMOND RAIN

may occur on **giant icy planets** such as **Neptune** and **Uranus,** thanks to the amount of **pressure** in their **atmospheres.**

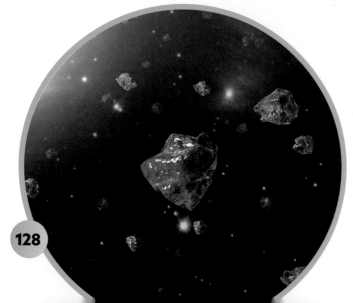

**ASTEROIDS** contain **valuable metals** like **nickel, platinum, cobalt** and **gold!** In the future, companies may use **asteroid mining** to get these **raw materials** from space!

## CRYSTAL RAIN

occurs on a **protostar** called **HOPS-68,** where **storms** of an **olive-green mineral** called **olivine** fall from the **sky.**

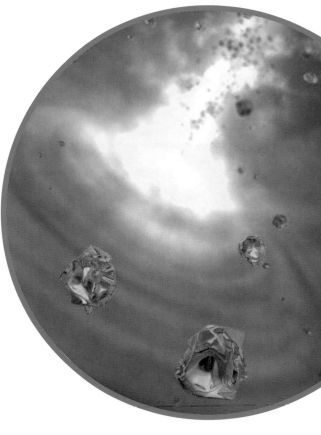

**HAT-P-7b** is a planet nicknamed **'Hot Jupiter'**, where the atmosphere is **so hot** that **clouds of corundum** (the mineral in **rubies** and **sapphires**) may be **blown across** the surface by **scorching winds.**

# a 'DAY' in the life of an ASTRONAUT

'Mornings' and 'evenings' don't really exist on an orbiting spacecraft, so astronauts have to set alarms that give structure to each of their 'days'.

Looking out of the window is one of the most popular ways astronauts spend their free time. They never get bored because the view is always changing!

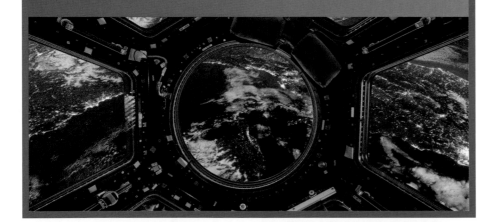

Magnets are used to stop knives and forks from floating off the table at meal times. Drinks and soups have to be sucked from plastic bags!

Washing your hair in space is surprisingly difficult! Space showers can't exist because the water would just float off without gravity! So, astronauts use a 'rinseless' shampoo.

Washing machines don't exist on board the International Space Station either! Instead, astronauts wear disposable clothes and replace them every three days or so – nice!

Sleeping bags need to be hooked to the walls each night to stop astronauts from floating away! Some astronauts say they start to dream of weightlessness.

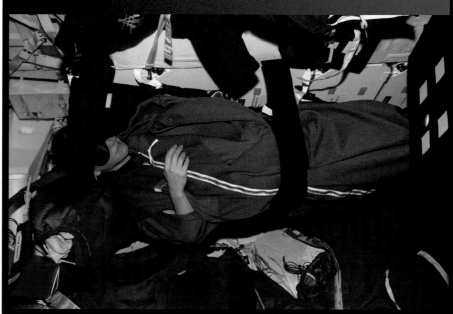

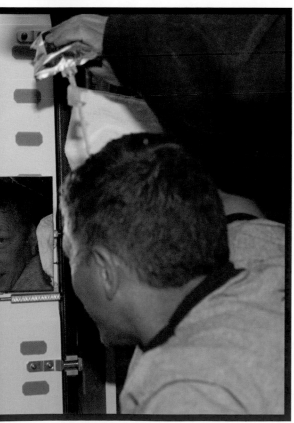

Returning to Earth can be difficult for astronauts. Spending so much time in space without gravity, means muscles become weak so they need special training to get back to nomral.

# Staggering
# SPACE-TIME

## WARNING:

These facts about space and time are absolutely mind-boggling!

**BLACK HOLES** could be massive enough to bend time. If someone could travel near a black hole, they would experience time much slower than someone back on Earth!

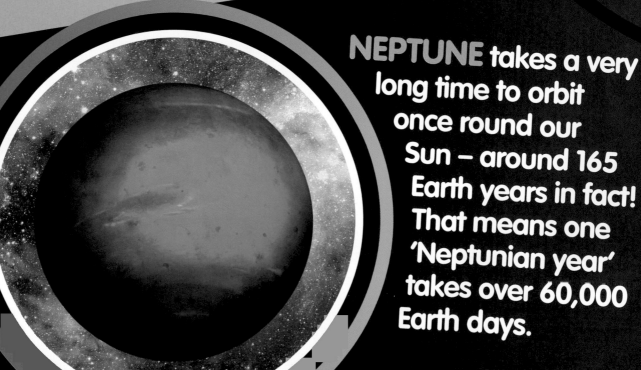

**NEPTUNE** takes a very long time to orbit once round our Sun – around 165 Earth years in fact! That means one 'Neptunian year' takes over 60,000 Earth days.

Over **65 MILLION YEARS AGO,** when dinosaurs were alive, there were around 23.5 hours in a day and 370 days in a year. Now, there are only 365 because the Moon's gravity is causing Earth to spin a little bit slower each day.

The **GROUNDHOG DAY SUPERNOVA** is a star that exploded in space over 9 billion years ago, but scientists have observed the event four times. Gravity from other galaxies caused light rays from the explosion to bend and reach Earth at different times, giving us many 'replays' of the same event.

# Sporting
# SUPERSTARS

While **STAND-UP PADDLE BOARDING** (SUP) only really took off in the **2000s**, people have been **FLOATING** and **SELF-PROPELLING** on boards for centuries. Combining **SUP AND YOGA**, however, is a modern sport that requires incredible **CORE STRENGTH.**

# CHAPTER 8

Reach out to page 144 for more activities that will make a splash.

# BRILLIANT BILES

**SIMONE BILES** is one of the **BEST GYMNASTS** of **ALL TIME!** She has an **INCREDIBLE** total of **30** (and counting) **OLYMPIC** and **WORLD CHAMPIONSHIP MEDALS** across the **VAULT, FLOOR, BEAM, UNEVEN BARS, ALL-ROUND** and **TEAM COMPETITIONS.**

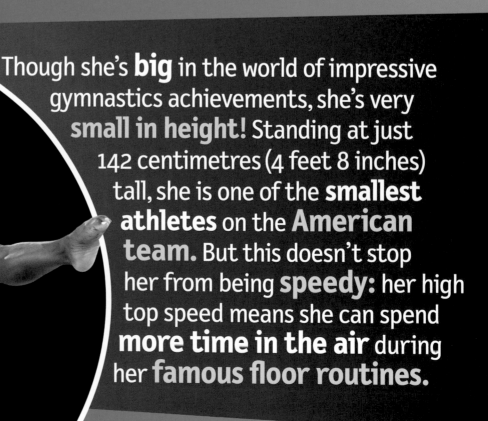

Though she's **big** in the world of impressive gymnastics achievements, she's very **small in height!** Standing at just 142 centimetres (4 feet 8 inches) tall, she is one of the **smallest athletes** on the **American team.** But this doesn't stop her from being **speedy:** her high top speed means she can spend **more time in the air** during her **famous floor routines.**

Her floor routines are so **awesome** that she has **invented** her own moves. The **'BILES'** is a **double twisting double backflip** and the **'BILES II'** a **triple twisting double backflip.**

**Simone** has such **great balance** and skill that she once took a **social media handstand challenge** to a whole new level by **taking off** her **tracksuit bottoms** with her **feet** while **standing** on her **hands** the whole time.

# In it for the LONG HAUL

*Would you have what it takes to compete in one of the longest races in the world!?*

THE TRANS-SIBERIAN **EXTREME** is known as the 'longest and toughest bicycle race in the world'. There are 15 stages, participants pass through five climate zones and eight time zones, totalling over 9,000 kilometres (5,592 miles) in 25 days.

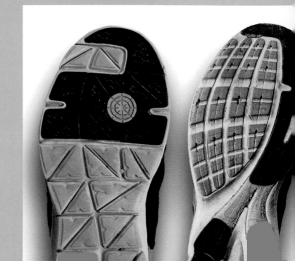

The **PATAGONIAN** >>>
**EXPEDITION RACE** is comprised of 9–14 days of **trekking**, sea kayaking, orienteering and **mountain biking**. Courses are up to 1,112 kilometres (691miles) and teams only discover the route 24 hours before the start.

The **SRI CHINMOY SELF-TRANSCENDENCE** is the longest footrace in the world. Participants have a maximum of 52 days to run 4,988 kilometres (3,100 miles), which is the distance from the west to the east coast of the USA plus 11 marathons! Runners have been known to go through 20 pairs of shoes!

The **OCEAN RACE** is a yacht race with one of the longest race routes in the world. Covering approximately 40,000 nautical miles, this race sees participants sail all around the globe!

# SWAPPING SPORTS

These sports superstars aren't just skilled in one sport, they've successfully switched it up!

**Pita Taufatofua** competed in **the Olympics** during his **Taekwondo career,** then in the Winter Olympics during his **skiing career.** He now competes in **sprint canoeing,** a sport that's close to his heart because of his **Polynesian heritage.**

## PITA TAUFATOFUA

## MILDRED DIDRIKSON

**Mildred Didrikson** had a successful career in **baseball** before she won two **track and field gold medals** at the **1932 Olympics.** She then became a **professional golfer** and won the **US Open** in **1948, 1950, 1954.**

**Dame Sarah Storey** won **16 Paralympic medals** (including five golds) for **swimming.** She then switched to **cycling** and won a further **nine medals,** all of them gold! Unsurprisingly, she is the **most successful British Paralympian** of all time.

**SARAH STOREY**

**Rebecca Romero** is the **first British athlete** to **win Olympic medals** in **different sports.** Rebecca started as a World Champion and Olympic **silver medal** winning **rower** and then **switched to cycling** where she won Olympic and World Championship **gold medals.**

**REBECCA ROMERO**

**PETR CECH**

**Petr Cech** is most famous for being a **football player.** He was one of the **best goalkeepers** in the **English Premier League,** before he **retired** and **switched** to playing in goal for an **ice hockey team!**

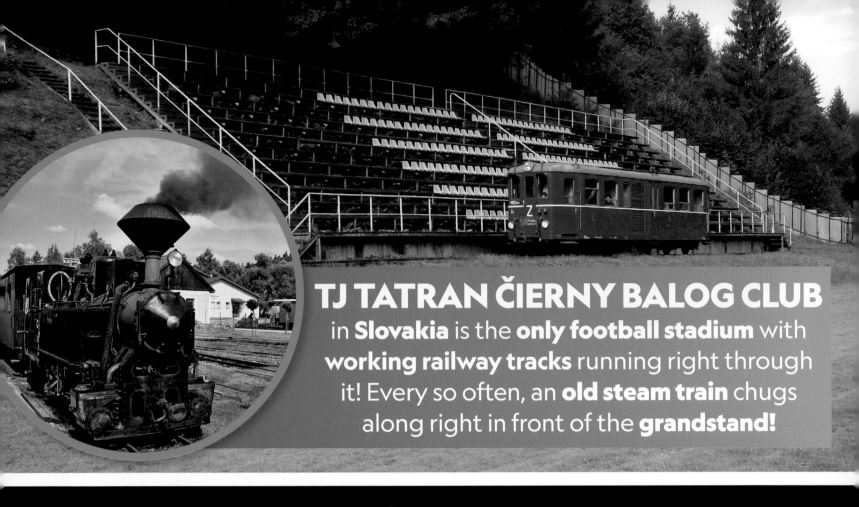

**TJ TATRAN ČIERNY BALOG CLUB**
in **Slovakia** is the **only football stadium** with **working railway tracks** running right through it! Every so often, an **old steam train** chugs along right in front of the **grandstand!**

# Seriously Strange

**THE FLOAT** is exactly what it sounds like: a **floating football pitch** in the middle of Marina Bay, **Singapore!** Games won't be interrupted by any pitch invaders here!

# BURSA BÜYÜKŞEHIR BELEDIYE STADIUM

in **Turkey** is nicknamed **'Timsah Arena'** which translates to **'Crocodile Arena'.** Can you guess why? It's designed to look like a **giant crocodile!**

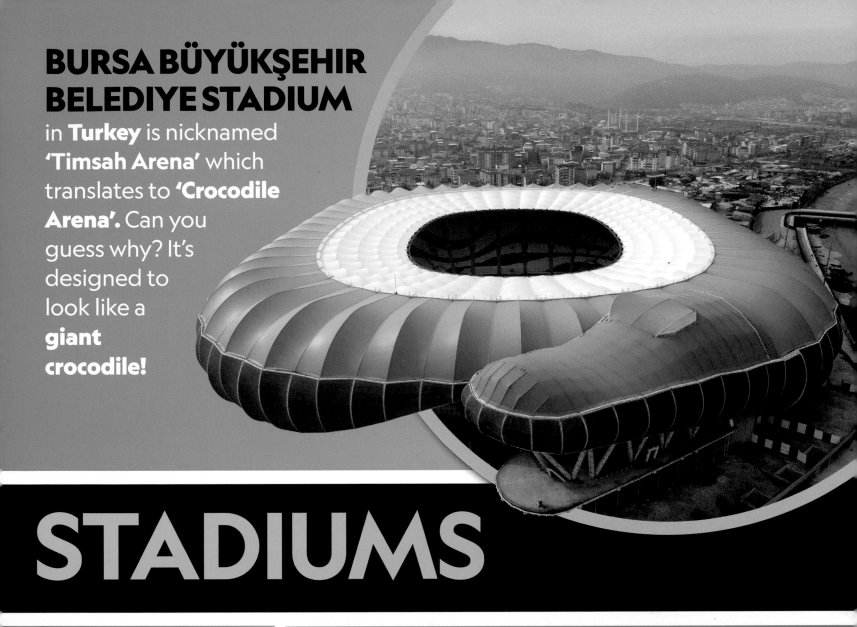

# STADIUMS

## TEVERSAL FC

in **England** use a **supermarket trolley park** as one of the **stands** in their football ground!

**AL-SHAMAL SC'S** home stadium was built to resemble a **traditional Qatari fortress.**

# Making a SPLASH

**Bare-foot water skiers** use their **feet** instead of **water-skis.**

>>>

**Stand-up paddleboard yoga** requires great balance – one wobble and you'll be in the water!

**Dragon boat racing** is a **Chinese tradition** of paddling **boats** shaped like **dragons** because dragons were believed to **control rivers.**

**Mud pit belly-flopping** is one of the **most popular contests** held during the **'Redneck Games'** in East Dublin, Georgia, USA.

SNUBA is a cross between **snorkelling** and **scuba diving!** Divers explore below the surface with extra-long air pipes.

^ ^ ^

**Kayaking over waterfalls** is a sport only attempted by the **craziest** of **daredevils.** Don't try this at home!

∨ ∨ ∨

**Water jetpack flying** makes you feel like a **superhero!** Jets of water **propel you into the air.**

**Octopush** is another name for **underwater hockey!** Fun to play but not so fun to watch!

∨ ∨ ∨

## 2,600 CALORIES

is the average amount of calories burned by a marathon runner during a race. That's the equivalent of around 10.5 hamburgers.

The **HIGHEST MARATHON** in the world is the Everest Marathon. The start line is **5,363 metres (17,595 feet)** above sea level.

In 2017, a **70-YEAR-OLD** woman ran **7 MARATHONS** on **7 CONTINENTS** in **7 DAYS.**

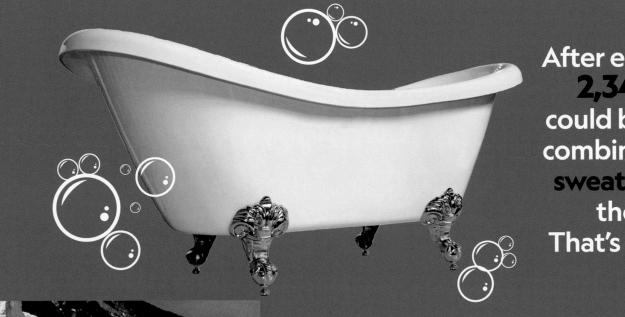

After each marathon, **2,340 BATHS** could be **filled by the** combined **amount of sweat** produced by the **runners.** That's a lot of sweat!

**SHISO KANAKURI** holds the **record** for the **slowest marathon.**

His time? **54 years, 246 days, 5 hours, 32 minutes,** and **20.3 seconds.**

After not finishing the race in **Stockholm in 1912** he was invited back to finish it **55 years later, in 1967.**

# SUPERHUMAN SWIMMER

**SARAH THOMAS** is the first person to swim the entire English Channel four times – **WITHOUT STOPPING!**

The distance was supposed to be around 129 kilometres (80 miles) long, but Sarah ended up swimming closer to 209 kilometres (130 miles) because of the tides that kept pulling her off track.

Such an epic swim took Sarah 54 hours to complete, meaning she swam for two days without sleeping!

It was tricky to get food and water to her while she was swimming constantly, so her mother had to tie protein drinks to a rope and throw them to her from a boat every 30 minutes!

Sarah was even stung by a jellyfish during her swim, but she still managed to soldier on!

After recently recovering from breast cancer, Sarah dedicated her ultra-marathon swim to other cancer survivors.

'STEPPING ON A SNAKE' is how **Kenyans** describe **missing the ball completely.**

# Funny
## Football
### PHRASES

A **'WARDROBE'** is what the **Spanish** call a tall, strong centre back!

Football fans all over the world have come up with some strange ways to describe specific parts of the 'beautiful game'.

A **'SALAD'** for **Jamaicans,** is what we might know as a **nutmeg** (kicking the ball through an opponents legs).

# Totally WEIRD!

'Pihkatappi' is a **Finnish** term for a defensive midfielder who **blocks the line** in front of the defence. This translates to 'poo plug'!

A **'BUTTER PASS'** is the **Swedish name** for a perfect pass that reaches the player **without them breaking stride.**

A **'BUTTERFLY HUNTER'** is what **Hungarians** call goalkeepers who try to **grab the ball** and **miss!**

**'WHERE THE OWL SLEEPS'** is what **Brazilians** call the **top corner of the goal.**

**'POSTMAN'** is the name given to **midfielders** in the **Netherlands** who make lots of short, **sideways passes.**

# Coolly CREATIVE

# CHAPTER 9

**VIVID SYDNEY** is Australia's largest festival and it attracts more than **2 MILLION** people every year. It started out as a light festival to promote ENERGY EFFICIENCY but is now one of the world's biggest **FESTIVALS** of light, music and ideas.

Power over to page 164 for more illuminating festival facts.

# swimming
## in the sky

# FESTIVAL OF THE WINDS is one of the world's biggest and best known kite festivals. For over 40 years, it has been taking place annually on Bondi Beach in Australia.

Over 70,000 kite-crazy visitors flock to see the skies fill up with HUGE, wacky kite creations, including creatures like koalas, whales, sharks, squids, and even Australia's famous redback spider!

When the festival started in 1978, there were only around 50 kites to see. Nowadays, there are closer to 500! Visitors also go along to watch dance performances by different cultural groups including Maori, Sri Lankan, and indigenous Australians!

The most **expensive painting** ever sold at auction was *Salvator Mundi (Saviour of the World)* by **LEONARDO DA VINCI**, which sold for over **£350 million!**

# PRICEY
## pieces

**COMEDIAN**

**A banana** duct-taped to a wall sold for **US$120,000** (£96,000) in 2019 at a prestigious art show in the **USA!** Despite the art installation being titled **'COMEDIAN'**, art critics insist that **MAURIZIO CATTELAN'S** creation is **no joke!**

This platinum sculpture of a human skull, encrusted with over 8,000 diamonds (and real human teeth!) cost artist **DAMIEN HIRST** around £14 million to make!

**LOUISE BOURGEOIS'** giant spider sculpture was installed at the **Guggenheim museum** in Spain for around **£9 million**. It's one of the most expensive art installations in recent history.

A **solid gold toilet worth over £4 million** was installed as an art exhibition at **Blenheim Palace in England**. Shortly afterwards, it was **stolen!** The loo must've been difficult to steal, as it weighed 103 kilograms (16.2 stone)!

The **CRWTH** is a **medieval folk instrument.** According to **legend,** a Welsh musician once *escaped* from a **pack of wolves** by **playing his crwth** for them!

# International INSTRUMENTS

The **BALALAIKA** is a **Russian instrument** developed in the **18th-century.** It has a **triangular wooden body** and *only three strings.* It's also known as a **Russian three stringed guitar!**

The **KOTO** is a **large wooden** instrument with **13 strings** strung out over **13 movable bridges!** It's the **national instrument** of Japan!

**TABLA** are **Indian hand drums.** Tabla players often learn a **'drum language'** to help them play, with words like *'na'*, *'tin'* *'tu'* and *'tete'* for different drum **strokes!**

The **MBIRA** is an **African thumb piano** which are sometimes made from **bike spokes, sofa springs** or other kinds of **recycled steel!**

The **HAEGŬM** is a traditional **Korean** instrument. It has a **long neck,** a hollow **wooden body,** and **two silk strings** that are played like a fiddle!

The **ANGKLUNG** is an **Indonesian** instrument made from various **bamboo tubes** on a **bamboo frame** that are **shaken** to play **different notes!**

# INVISIBLE HOMEWORK!?

Japanese student of ninja history, Eimi Haga, initially caused confusion when she handed in a blank essay paper to her professor. Luckily, she had left a note in the corner that said 'heat the paper'. Once heated over the stove, her essay began to appear!

As it turned out, she had used a technique called 'aburidashi', which was traditionally used by ninjas to send secret messages!

The process included spending hours crushing and soaking soybeans just to make a special invisible ink that only appears when heated up, then using a fine brush to write the entire essay onto Japanese washi paper.

Do you think 'they're not blank pages, I wrote it in invisible ink!' will become the new 'my dog ate my homework'?

Of course, Eimi's professor was very impressed and she received TOP MARKS for her essay!

100%

# CRAZY CAREERS

**SNAKE MILKERS** are brave zoologists who collect venom from snakes and other poisonous reptiles for use in anti-venom medicines!

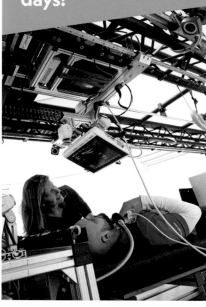

**PROFESSIONAL BED TESTERS** were hired by NASA to lie in bed for up to 60 days!

**AMEZAIKU ARTISTS** are professional Japanese sculptors of sweets that create intricate artworks from sugar and edible dyes!

**PROFESSIONAL MERMAIDS** are hired to swim and perform in full mermaid costumes, complete with tails!

**OSHIYAS** are hired in Japan to push passengers onto extremely crowded trains during rush hours!

**HOLLYWOOD CREATURE PERFORMERS** are hired to play a wide range of characters, including animals and monsters!

**THE RAVENMASTER** of the Tower of London has to look after six ravens that supposedly 'protect the Kingdom of England'!

**GLOBEMAKERS** have the weight of the world in their hands... literally! They hand craft spheres and turn them into globes!

**BODY PAINTERS** specialise in creating full body designs; they usually work at fun events like festivals and fairs!

# FANTASTIC FESTIVALS

**Vivid Sydney** is a **festival of light, music and ideas** that lights up **Sydney, Australia...** *literally!* Huge **light installations** are **projected** onto some of the city's most famous buildings!

Sydney Opera House

## Totally **WEIRD!**

**Wave-Gotik-Treffen** in **Germany** is the biggest **goth festival** in the world, celebrating all things gothic, including **'dark music'**, **'dark culture'** and some **creepy costumes!**

## KETTLEWELL SCARECROW FESTIVAL

**Kettlewell Scarecrow Festival** is one of the longest-running scarecrow festivals in the world! Thousands of people come to see this small English village completely transformed by straw characters!

## BUSÓJÁRÁS

**Busójárás** is an annual festival held in the **Hungarian town** of Mohács, where the town is taken over by men in coats and masks, scaring away winter!

## WORLD BODYPAINTING FESTIVAL

**The World Bodypainting Festival** in **Austria** is a colourful occasion that celebrates the human body being used as a canvas for all kinds of incredible masterpieces!

# FULLY BOOKED

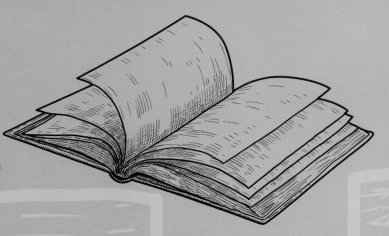

The **BROOKLYN ART LIBRARY** in New York City, USA, is neither a **traditional library** nor an **art gallery** – it's a **mixture** of both! It is home to **the Sketchbook Project,** where **thousands** of people send a sketchbook in the **mail** so it can live in the **art library forever,** on display to thousands of **strangers!**

For over 10 years, creative people from all over the world have been sending in their sketchbooks to be put on the shelves. All kinds of people have contributed, from professional illustrators and painters to children and first-time artists. There are now over 40,000 sketchbooks in the collection, from over 130 countries, making it the world's largest collection of artist sketchbooks.

**Sketchbooks at Brooklyn Art Library**

And it might just be the world's most unique collection of art too, as each sketchbook is filled with completely different kinds of artwork from drawings, doodles and sketches to writing, collages, and poetry!

When the sketchbooks reach the art library, they are sorted into a category depending on what's inside. Visitors can flip through any sketchbook they like, opening the door to a stranger's world of thoughts, feelings and artwork.

WIDE AWAKE CRESCENT SHAPED SMILE

## Totally **WEIRD!**

Some **art-loving couples** have got **married** among the **sketchbooks.**

# Grub's UP!

# CHAPTER 10

BUDDHA'S HAND fruits come in different VARIETIES, but the main difference is that some come as 'OPEN-HAND' varieties, where their segments stretch OUTWARDS, whereas others are 'CLOSED-HAND', meaning their 'FINGERS' stay closed together.

**Feast your eyes on page 170 for more facts about freaky fruits.**

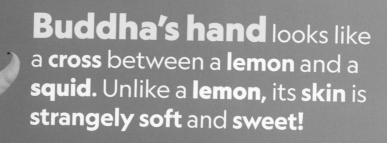

**Buddha's hand** looks like a **cross** between a **lemon** and a **squid**. Unlike a **lemon**, its **skin** is strangely **soft** and **sweet!**

# Freaky
# FRUITS

**Pitaya,** or **dragon fruit,** grows on **cacti** and is known for its **bright colours.** It's **pollinated** by **nocturnal creatures** such as **moths** and **bats.**

**Rambutans** are closely related to **lychees.** Their **spiky perm** gives them a **distinctive look** and their name comes from the **Malay** word **'rambut'** meaning **'hair'.**

**Hala fruit** looks like an **exploding planet!** Because it **rots quickly** in the sun it also goes by the name **'stink nut'**!

**Gac fruit** is a **rare** and **creamy** fruit. It is used as part of a **ceremonial Vietnamese wedding dish** because it turns the **rice orange.**

**Miracle berry** has a **unique super power:** it can **change** how other foods taste! It makes **sour foods** taste **sweet.**

**Ackee fruit** tastes just like **cream cheese!** Beware, the rest of the fruit pod is **very poisonous** and causes **vomiting.**

**Jabuticaba's** name comes from the **Tupi** (extinct Brazilian language) **word** meaning **'tortoise place'.** It grows very close to the **tree trunk** making it look like it's wrapped in **purple bubble-wrap!**

# A FEAST fit for a QING

The **MANCHU–HAN IMPERIAL FEAST** was one of the **grandest banquets** ever documented **in history**. Taking place in the Qing dynasty (1644–1912) of **China** to celebrate the **66th birthday** of the Qing Emperor Kangxi, this **gigantic ceremonial feast** was spread out into **six banquets, over three days!**

It wasn't just the length of the **feast** that was **impressive;** over **2,500 guests** attended this gastronomic celebration, sampling an array of **fine cuisine.**

**Emperor Kangxi**

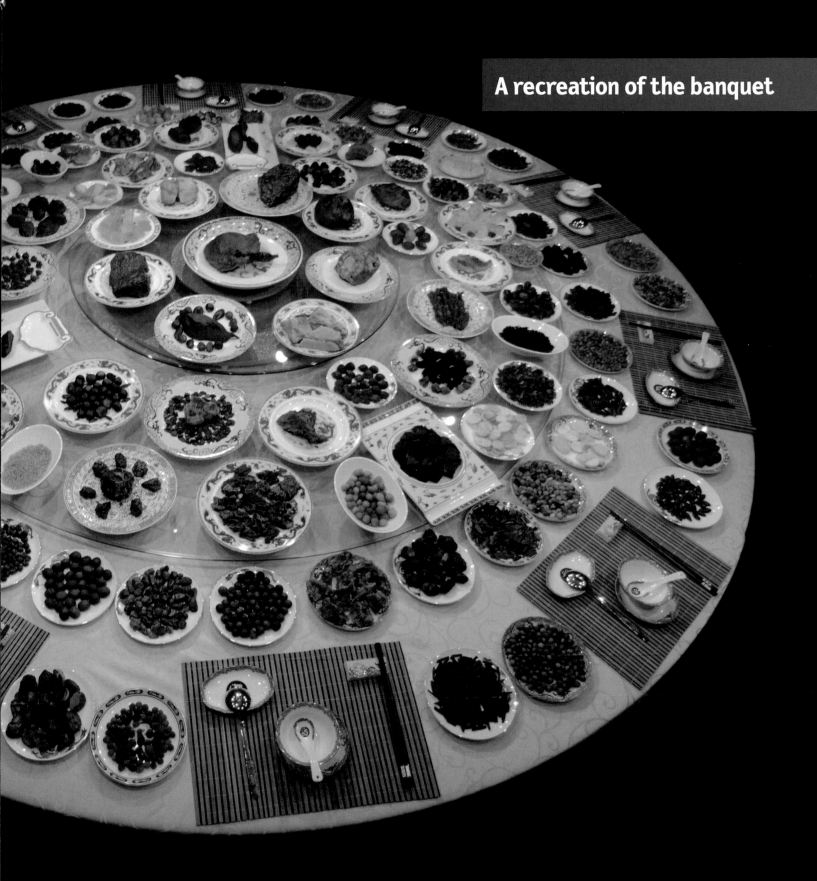

These dishes were served on **lavish bronze** and **porcelain tableware,** often shaped like animals and designed with special mechanisms to keep the food warm throughout the banquet.

# CHEESE
## the DAY

**7** cheerfully cheese-tastic facts you didn't know!

## ROQUEFORT
is a blue cheese that gets its flavour from a kind of mould that grows in the Mont Combalou caves of Southern France.

A **TUROPHILE** is someone who **LOVES** CHEESE.

CHEDDAR CHEESE ICE CREAM is a favourite in **the Philippines!**

**CASU MARZU** is a seriously stinky **Sardinian** cheese that's **infested** with live **maggots** and is **illegal** in many countries!

The **largest cheese platter** ever made weighed over **2,000 kilograms** and had a whopping **145** varieties of cheese!

**TYROMANCY** was the **ancient art** of **predicting** the **future** by observing cheese as it **curdled.**

**PULE** is one of the most **expensive** cheeses in the **world.** It's made from **donkey milk** and costs over **£800** per kilogram!

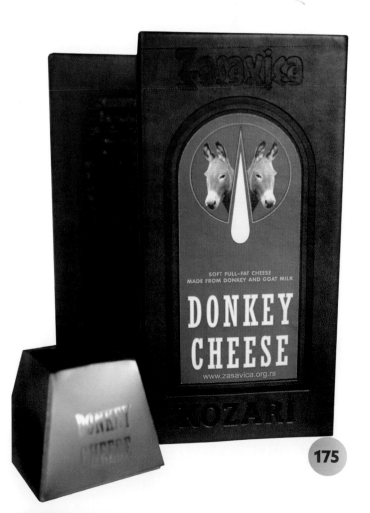

**CHEESE-COVERED DOUGHNUTS,** yes, that's right: **sugar-glazed doughnuts** sprinkled with **cheddar** and **Swiss cheese.**

# IN THE MOOD FOR FAST FOOD?

**THE RAMEN BURGER** has a **teriyaki, soy** or **shoyu flavour burger** and instead of **bread buns,** it's made with two **pan-fried discs** of **ramen noodles!**

**THE KURO NINJA** is a burger made to look like a **cartoon ninja. 'Kuro'** is **Japanese** for 'black' and this burger certainly is. The meat is encased in **black burger buns,** with **black cheese** and **black ketchup!**

**FISH CEVICHE (raw fish** with **citrus juices** and **spices)** is served up as fast food in **Nicaragua.**

These **wacky food items** have been served in some of the **most popular fast food shops** in the world...

**LOBSTER ROLLS** are **fast food sandwiches** filled with **lobster meat** on a bed of lettuce inside a toasted roll. Served with a **slice of lemon**, this is **fast food** with a **fancy twist!**

# Home SWEET Home

A **gingerbread city** is created **every year** in **Bergen, Norway.**

The German city of Nuremburg is known as the 'Gingerbread capital of the World'.

The **word** 'gingerbread' comes from the **French** word 'gingebras' which means 'preserved ginger'.

In **SWEDEN,** there is a **tradition** where people **snap** gingerbread biscuits when **making a wish.**

The **largest gingerbread house** ever built was in **Texas, USA,** and was over **18 metres** (60 feet) long and **3 metres** (10 feet) tall. This **colossal creation** used a whopping **7,200 eggs!**

## Totally **WEIRD!**

Overall, the building contained **36 million calories.** To put that into perspective, you would need to run over **13,000 marathons** to burn that off!

It is believed that **Queen Elizabeth I** came up with the original **gingerbread man concept,** using them as **gifts** to **visitors.**

179

# ON A ROLL!

## LOVE SUSHI?
Love burgers? Why not try the **fabulous fusion** that is the **sushi burger?**

## SUSHI BAZOOKAS
are **kitchen gadgets** that fire out roll after roll of **perfect sushi pieces!**

Ever wished your sushi was a **different shape?** Doughnut worry, **sushi doughnuts** now exist!

**MOSAIC SUSHI** blends the **art of sushi** and mosaic-making into one delicious craft.

**GELATO SUSHI** are ice-cream desserts shaped like sushi pieces, sometimes served with sweet, spicy chocolate wasabi!

**TAMA-CHAN** is a Japanese 'illustrator-chef' who creates incredible sushi artworks and teaches classes in sushi art.

# The colour PURPLE

CARROTS

**WHO SAID VEGETABLES NEED TO BE DULL?**
These **FANTASTIC FOODS** aren't just **COLOURFUL** – they are really good for your **HEALTH**, too.

CAULIFLOWER

**PURPLE CAULIFLOWERS** get their tinge from an antioxidant called anthocyanin. As well as providing a **punchy purple colour**, the **antioxidants** are great for your body.

ASPARAGUS

If **GREEN ASPARAGUS** is usually off the menu, why not switch to the purple variety? These super spears are more tender and much **sweeter**.

Most people are familiar with **orange carrots,** but these vivid veggies come in a **spectrum of colours** including **black, red, white,** yellow and **purple.**

BROCCOLI

**PURPLE BROCCOLI** has grown in popularity in recent years. It has a more nutty and **peppery** taste compared to the traditional green variety.

The humble spud may have a reputation for being boring, but **PURPLE POTATOES** can liven up your dinner plate and may even be **healthier** than regular potatoes.

POTATOES

# DON'T PLAY with your FOOD!

We all know we're not supposed to play with our food, but through playing around with experiments, scientists have created some amazing things! Check out these fascinating food modifications...

## VENOMOUS CABBAGE

might be the secret to preventing crop damage without using pesticides. Researchers are experimenting with a poison found in scorpion tails that can deter caterpillars but is harmless to humans!

## GENETICALLY ENGINEERED TOMATOES that

have the scent of lemon and rose have been created by scientists in Israel.

**LETTUCE** modified with the **INSULIN** gene may one day provide a **veggie-tastic** cure for **diabetes!** Some of the scientific experiments with this lettuce so far have had **positive results** when tested.

Insulin

**SQUARE APPLES** and **BUDDHA-SHAPED PEARS** now exist thanks to a company in China that creates special fruit moulds. They also created moulds to grow heart-shaped watermelons!

# Index

# Image credits